Passport Parenting

By Zoë Ledsham

Copyright © 2024, Zoë Ledsham

All rights reserved.

No part of this publication may be reproduced, distributed, or transmitted in any form or by any means, including photocopying, recording, or other electronic or mechanical methods, without the prior written permission of the author.

Printed and bound in Great Britain.

First edition 2024

ISBN: 9798326947673

For Evelyn Skye, without you there would be no adventure.

For Mumsy, I love you millions & squillions. Thank you for everything.

"The world is a book, and those who don't travel only read one page."

— St. Augustine

Note from the Author

I never intended to write this book. It wasn't on my list of things I would accomplish during my lifetime. If you'd have told me in 2019 that I would be writing a book at all, I'd have laughed. If you told me I'd be writing a book about what I have learnt on my parenting journey, I would have been speechless with disbelief. No chance. Not me.

I wasn't sure that I would have any children, let alone be sharing the experience with the world and highlighting my parenting mishaps for the entertainment of others. But here we are.

Somewhere along the way, amongst the dramatic voice notes to loved ones and hurried entries in journals, this book was written.

I hope you enjoy it.

Contents:

1. Passport Parenting 10
2. Me Before You..17
3. WTF Do We Do Now? 27
4. Benefits of Travelling with Babies 34
5. Shared Parental Leave.......................................38
6. 12 Countries in 12 Months.................................43
7. Travel Friendly Destinations...............................47
8. Preparing for the Journey: Packing.....................54
9. Health & Safety..63
10. Navigating Airports & Flights.............................74
11. Accommodation..81
12. Daily Routines & Managing Schedules..................90
13. Coping with Stress...96
14. Cultural Immersion & Language Development........101
15. Travel Tales..109
16. Budgeting & Financial Tips................................128
17. Technology, Tools & Resources...............................135
18. Different Types of Travel: Rural vs City................140
19. Seasonal Travel...146
20. Long Term Travel & Working Remotely.................152
21. What Next? 159
22. Conclusion...161
23. Recommendations..162
24. Final Word..... 168
25. Appendix 1: Sample Packing List........................169
26. Appendix 2: Travel Checklist.............................172

Chapter 1

Passport Parenting – what is it all about?

In short, I wrote this book because it is the book I wish that I could have read before I had my baby. It is a book that endeavours to show you all the wonderful possibilities there are for travelling with your baby and the opportunities that this new chapter of your life will bring.

The message of this book is simple: you can travel with your baby. You absolutely **can** do it.

Will it be chaotic? Probably. Stressful? Possibly. Unforgettable? Definitely.

Now, I am by no means an expert on this topic, or on parenting in general for that matter. In many ways, we are the blind leading the blind on this one. It is also worth mentioning that I am doing parenting on what some would call 'easy mode' – I only have one child. For those of you who do this with more than one child and just two hands, you are wizards.

With that being said, by sharing my experience my hope is that this will motivate and encourage others who are considering travelling with their babies but are concerned about how it might look in reality vs what you see people doing on social media.

On this journey there will be some highs, some lows, some laughs and some lessons learned. But the good news is, I've done a lot of the parenting cockups for you already so you can save yourself the headache.

A lot of the information that I was given, and books that I was bought when I announced that I was pregnant, seemed written to warn me, change me and terrify me in equal measure. Now, I know that it is important to be informed. Pregnancy can be a very anxious time and the idea of having a guidebook and an endless stream of information at your fingertips is very reassuring.

With that being said, the amount of conflicting information about routines, sleep training and weaning guides can be overwhelming and leave you thinking that parenting is a test that you are going to fail. It can feel like everybody else knows best and you need to get up to speed. Quickly. It can leave you feeling as though your life is no longer your own and everything will completely change. And it does. Of course, you have to entirely shift your priorities and how you usually do things to accommodate your new little baby who depends on you.

However, what seems to be lacking from a lot of this literature is how you can **adapt** your life to accommodate your new baby. You don't have to overhaul and change everything you know and enjoy. You do not need to change from somebody who enjoys a glass of wine at a little beach bar at the weekend into somebody who only spends their Sundays mass producing organic finger food for the week ahead.

You do not need to immediately take up residence in parent and toddler groups and baby sensory classes if you don't want to. There are other ways to help your baby develop and let your baby experience the world around them. There is no 'one size fits all' approach to parenting. You don't need to make your own world smaller for your baby to thrive.

However, a lot of these groups are also designed to help new parents connect with other parents and expand their social and support networks. That can be something extremely beneficial and a lot of my own friends have made lifelong friends at these groups. I am fortunate that a lot of my friends have babies already, so I get to spend time with my favourite people and let the kids entertain themselves. I'm a terrible hostess so our friends Melissa and Richy do most of the heavy lifting in the hosting department for our other friends and I. They have two kids under 4 and their house is always immaculate, even if you call round unannounced. It is very annoying.

When I was pregnant, I was very concerned about how my life would change and whether I would be able to still go on holiday occasionally. Would it now be impossible? Too stressful? Too much to pack to take with us? It was none of those things. Stressful at times, sure. Too stressful? Definitely not. It can be stressful going to Sainsburys with a baby so if I have to choose where I'd rather be stressed, it will always be on a beach.

I felt compelled to write this book to inform, encourage and motivate those of you who are looking to get out there with your babies and young children to explore the world. For me, it is such an important message to get out there to people. People are often so surprised when they ask me on the plane or at the airport: 'is this your daughter's first flight?' and I say 'no, it's her 25th'.

As I have travelled with my daughter over the past 18 months, I have encountered so many people on planes, on the beach, on social media and everywhere in between who have asked me what it's like travelling with such a young baby, how do we do it? And (most of all) how do we manage with a couple of small backpacks and a fold-up pram?

Now, like you, I am a keen traveller. Always have been. I love to visit other countries, learn about other cultures, try new foods and experience new things. Throughout my life I have always been a keen linguist, and I have always made the most of any opportunity to learn a new language or develop my existing skills. Travelling has always been a great way to do this.

Over the past few years, I have spent as much time abroad as time and money would allow. It became a running joke with my friends and family and whenever they saw me, they would ask 'how long are you in the country for this time?'. The answer was always 'not for long if I can help it!'. For me, travelling has always been something that I am passionate about, and I have loved having the freedom to travel and explore the world.

After spending my time eating pasta in Rome, whale watching in Canada and sunning myself on beaches in Greece without a care in the world…suddenly, I blinked and somehow ended up in my late twenties. The horror. During this period, more and more of my friends were settling down, buying houses and having their lovely children. My stepsisters and my stepbrother had all had children by this point as well and they were a similar age to me. I was simultaneously very excited for them and terrified for me. When did we become grownups, please? Were we in our 'having a baby era' and nobody had told me?

Whenever I thought about having children, though I wasn't against having them, I was paralysed with the fear that having a child would close the adventure chapter of my life. My misguided perception was that I wouldn't get to have a life of my own anymore and I wouldn't experience the thrill of going somewhere new or watching the sunset on a beautiful beach, for quite some time.

My Mum had me when she was just 16 years old and of course, as I grew up it was just normal to me that I had a young mum. I didn't really think anything of it. However, as I got older, and especially as I turned 16 myself, I was absolutely stunned that my Mum had managed to have and raise a baby at that age. She had my brother, Jacob, at 21 and then graduated from university. The woman is a superhero and I have so much respect for her. As I now have a baby of my own, and just one baby at that, I truly don't know how she managed to do all that and work with two small children in tow. I was 32 when I had Evelyn and still do not feel like I am grown up enough to have a child. I am in constant awe of what women can achieve.

When I fell pregnant with my daughter in 2021, one thing that struck me, after the initial excitement and congratulations, was how often people would gleefully tell me that my wings had been clipped and that my travelling days were over. Bad luck. It's playgroups, weaning charts and baby sensory classes for you! I found it very irritating at the time and I lost count of the amount of (well-meaning?) people that said this to me during pregnancy and in the early days after Evelyn was born.

Unfortunately, what I've just described is often how people see it when you choose to have a child, that your opportunity to travel and experience the world is effectively over until your child is grown up. There's an unspoken expectation that you will now stay home and be unable to enjoy anything that you used to before you had your baby. Your life will now be dictated by naptimes and the busy schedule of Peppa Pig.

Now that I have had some time to reflect on this period, and now that my initial rage has subsided, I do think a lot of this comes down to people's own experiences. It is more about how comfortable they would feel or have felt about the prospect of travelling and less about placing limitations on you. Regardless, the loud and abrasive message I received from a lot of other parents was this: if I couldn't do it, you can't either.

After hearing that my travelling days were numbered, I went into panic mode and I booked a number of trips. I travelled abroad every month that I was pregnant except for September, when Evelyn was born.

As a result, during my pregnancy I spent time in Canada, France, Mallorca, Italy, Denmark, the USA and everywhere in between. We spent a month travelling around the USA and Canada on an epic road trip when I was 6 months pregnant and had a brilliant time. Granted the 10-mile hike in Yosemite in 35-degree heat was ill advised on reflection but the views were something else. On the last night of that trip, as I sipped my alcohol-free cocktail in Las Vegas, I thought to myself, this is it. My final hurrah. This is me saying goodbye to the independent, frequent flier that I am, and I was set to put my passport away in the drawer to gather dust until Evelyn turned 18 years old.

However, Evelyn is now 18 months old and, at the time I'm writing this to you, she has been to 18 countries and doesn't plan on slowing down yet.

I wrote this book with one aim, to challenge the misconception that your life is over when you have a child. To tell you, frankly, that it's bollocks. It may look a little different than before, you may have more luggage and feel more frazzled than before, but travelling isn't over for you.

In fact, the adventure is just beginning.

Chapter 2

Me Before You

Before I had Evelyn, I had a whole other life of my own. It feels like a distant memory to me now of course, but the highlights in my camera roll occasionally remind me that I was person all my own. Before I was Mummy.

I lived in London for the majority of my twenties, moving there from the Wirral (near Liverpool for those who haven't had the pleasure) in 2013. Whilst I was in London, I studied law and subsequently qualified as a lawyer and went onto work in the City amongst the corporate chaos. It was exactly as you might imagine it, less glamorous than Suits, but with long hours, lots of work and little sleep. The industry at that time was heavily based around the 'work hard, play hard' culture and aside from the long hours we'd spend working, we'd spend just as many drinking and networking. It was a lot of fun, a lot of stress and, unsurprisingly, very expensive. Regardless, I had a great time whilst living in London and made some good memories, some hazy ones and some lifelong friends along the way.

During this period Mike was also studying in London and he was at medical school training as a doctor. His life also consisted of many long hours, a lot of work and little sleep, though (thankfully) without the excess of booze that my profession encouraged at that point.

Throughout our time in London, we didn't travel as much as we'd like as we were focused on studying, working and paying London rent. We had the mindset of, we can do it later. We have loads of time, we'll focus on our careers first.

In the summer of 2020, in the height of the COVID-19 pandemic, we moved out of Surrey, where we'd spent the final couple of years and into Manchester. At this stage we had both got new jobs and Mike was going to be working in Manchester for the next couple of years. At that point it seemed like a good move for us at the time and because of everything going on with COVID-19 we were keen to be closer to our families that we had been unable to see for months.

During that COVID summer, I had my 30th birthday. In June 2020, I stationed myself in a local park where people had to come and visit me on a specific schedule and remain socially distanced (naturally). A truly bizarre time when I look back on it now, but I feel very fortunate that I was able to see my parents, my siblings, friends and, most importantly, my grandparents. Granted we were all terrified of passing COVID-19 to them, so the event was punctuated with some anxiety, despite the social distancing.

In June 2021 my lovely Gran, my Dad's mother, passed away suddenly from a stroke a couple of days after her 81st birthday and we were devastated. After this had happened, I reflected on a phone call I'd had with her a couple of weeks earlier where she told me that I needed to get out there and see the world now that it was open again post COVID. She'd told me she was really looking forward to going back to visit Javea in Spain, where she'd lived for many years. We had a family trip booked for that October, but sadly she never got to go back.

Her death refocused my priorities and made me think about the things I wanted to do and see but hadn't had the chance to yet. We always assume that tomorrow is guaranteed, and you can put things off until later. But tomorrow isn't guaranteed. After this reality check, I chose to spend the rest of the summer abroad in Spain, Malta and Cyprus.

When I came back, the travelling bug had truly taken hold and I then spent 5 weeks in Italy throughout September and October travelling around with my friend Lizzie. We went from boats in Venice to Vespas in Lake Garda, to Portofino and beyond. I'm not entirely convinced we should have been on the Italian motorway on our electric scooter, but it was an experience. By the time I came back to the UK in the autumn, I was feeling better and more positive. I had for the most part, processed my grief and during this period I'd been able to experience a lot of new countries, cultures and, most importantly, foods.

As we came into the Christmas period, I was understandably very keen to see the back of 2021 and start afresh with a new year. Now, as a side note I am somebody who absolutely loves New Year. I like to write lists of accomplishments from the previous year and set goals for the next. I do appreciate that it is perhaps the most hated event on the calendar for most people. Anyway, there we are in the festive season, deep in tinsel and mulled wine. It is Christmas Eve. I am in a restaurant sipping red wine and panicking about my last-minute wrapping when I get the call from my brother. My Grandad, my Mum's Dad, passed away suddenly about an hour ago. Our world is rocked again.

This was the worst Christmas on record for our family and I don't know how we got through it honestly. I remember sitting at my Mum's table on Christmas Day poking at my turkey wondering how on earth we were still attempting to have a Christmas at all. My Grandad notoriously hated Christmas and would wear one of those 'Bah Humbug' Christmas hats every year. This was particularly hilarious to me because my Grandma, conversely, absolutely loves Christmas and will begin planning for it in August. He certainly chose to go out with a bang and make his dislike for the festive season clear one final time by leaving us on Christmas bloody Eve.

A couple of days later, just before New Years' Eve, I got the news that Claudia, one of my close friends from London, had tragically been found dead in her flat at 37 years old.

Well, they say that things come in threes, and I was truly done for the year, just in time for Auld Lang Syne to see us out of 2021. Thank God.

I found out that I was pregnant with Evelyn just before New Year and although I fell pregnant with Evelyn at a *very* turbulent time in my life, I was surprisingly quite excited when I got the news. Even though I hadn't been planning to have a baby and was largely still on the fence about the idea, as I set out at the start of this book. However, I think getting pregnant at the time that I did was very fortuitous and felt like a glimmer of light in an otherwise very dark period for me personally and for our family.

When I shared the news that I was expecting a baby, everybody was absolutely stunned. Perhaps as stunned as I was honestly. Everybody was thrilled for us and, as predicted, my Mum went into obsessive baby mode almost immediately.

Because I was concerned about not being able to travel anymore once our baby arrived, I set about organising several trips before she made her debut. The following month Mike and I went to Lanzarote for a week where we went on boat trips to watch dolphins and lazed by the pool. We also attempted to go diving but the instructor promptly informed me that as a pregnant person I was now a protected species and unable to go. Mike, being the supportive individual that he is, promptly left me with the bags and went off into the sea with the instructor. Livid, I went off in a sulk to the nearest bar with a table in the sun and sipped San Miguel zeros in a rage until he returned a couple of hours later. The benefit of the all-inclusive on that trip was entirely lost on me, but I got my money's worth in desserts and Fanta lemon.

A few weeks later I took myself off to Copenhagen for a long weekend as I'd never been, and it was a relatively inexpensive last-minute trip. Copenhagen was lovely and I would recommend it as a weekend destination. It's got some brilliant cafés, bars and restaurants. It also has a food market in the centre which was excellent for small bites to eat, breakfasts and purchasing various deli items, fruit and flowers. Whilst I was in Copenhagen, one of my friends from London, Thomas, got in touch to say he was living in Malmo, Sweden now, and he could be in Copenhagen within the hour to meet me. I met him in a little indie café not far from the train station and we caught up on life. I hadn't announced to the world that I was pregnant at this point, so I was subtly ordering non-alcoholic beer and pour the jaeger shots he was buying us into the plants on the middle of the table. I think I got away with it…

The following month, I went to Paris for a few days with my three friends and luckily at this point I had started telling people that I was pregnant. I watched enviously as they sipped lovely French wines and ate all the amazing cheeses that were sadly off the menu for me. I visit Paris every year and have done since 2010, it is one of my favourite cities to visit.

For me, it is such an interesting city with so many different neighbourhoods and a different vibe in each. I never get bored of it and find new places that I love each time I go. Usually, however, I go there with the intention of sampling some of France's finest wines so going there and sipping sparkling water was a sobering experience in more ways than one. Suddenly the people stumbling out of wine bars on a Friday night seemed slightly less chic and charmant to me than they did under the warm afterglow of a pinot noir.

Despite my limited beverage options, I had a brilliant time and made up for the shortfall of grapes in crêpes and various tasty pastries across the city. I will say that it was an interesting choice for us all to go to Disneyland Paris on this trip as, as a pregnant person, I was banned from pretty much every ride except the Winnie the Pooh ride.

I think I spent 90 euros to get into the park, another 15 euros on sequin Minnie Mouse ears and then spent the morning waiting for my friends to queue up for and go on rides. After I was nearly mowed down in the middle of Main Street by a sparkly blue float with Elsa singing on top of it, I decided to cut my losses and go to Montmartre. I left my friends queueing for Space Mountain and made my escape. I had a lovely time roaming the streets of Montmartre, eating my way through the patisseries of Paris and purchasing gift boxes of macarons I would almost definitely eat on the 50-minute flight home.

A day before I was due to return from Paris, Mike called me to tell me that his Grandma, affectionately known as Franma, had passed away suddenly. We were suddenly quite thin on the ground for grandparents. We'd lost three in less than a year and were really upset that none of them had lived long enough to meet Evelyn.

My Grandma, Val, is the only grandparent we have left now and much as I would like to wrap her in bubble wrap and not let her leave the house, she's the one who passed the travel bug down to me. She is unstoppable and can often be found travelling around India, on a cruise to the Norwegian fjords and everything in between. Her favourite place to go is Greece and she lived out there with my Grandad for a couple of years but is always going back for a visit. She is never in the country, she's worse than I am for booking a trip.

A few weeks after I came back from Paris, after Franma's funeral, I went to Mallorca for a couple of weeks. After my previous pregnant adventures and the stress of recent events, I decided to take it easy on this trip and embrace the slower way of life. I spent a lot of time on the beach and eating paella. My friend Zoë came out to meet me there and we had a lovely few days sunning ourselves and enjoying Palma. As I watched her drinking various mojitos and shouting in sports bars whilst I had another Fanta lemon, I considered that I was perhaps having the longest pregnancy of all time. And I still had another 5 months to go.

After I returned from Mallorca, Mike and I got organised for our Big Trip. We had decided to spend 4 weeks travelling around the USA and Canada. Our plan was to fly into Vancouver and make our way down into the States, hire a car and meander down the West Coast.

We landed in Vancouver, which was a very cool place, we visited Granville Island where a seagull got caught in my hair and snatched my doughnut out of my hand in all the commotion. We stayed there for a few days and then made our way down into Seattle, which was as rainy as I'd anticipated.

For reasons unknown, I thought it would be a great idea to book a sunset boat cruise in Seattle. When we turned up for our boat cruise, the rain was torrential, and I was dressed for summer. I told myself it was character building, so we climbed aboard and got chatting to one of the crew onboard, Noah. We told him all about our big plans for the road trip and the route we had planned out. He told us to change the route immediately and make sure that we went via the Redwood Forest on our way through California. We took his advice and changed our plans. He was completely right.

We continued into California and spent a couple of days exploring Yosemite which, whilst absolutely breathtaking, was perhaps not the wisest choice for someone now 6 months pregnant in 38-degree heat. We walked for miles, and I was absolutely exhausted by the time that we left. I would recommend Yosemite to anybody; it truly is such a special place and I wish we'd had more time there. From there we went to San Francisco, Big Sur, LA and then drove to Vegas. Mike had never been to Vegas before and it's fair to say that he was completely floored by it.

By the time we returned from our trip to the States, I was quite pregnant but still determined to travel. So, solo again, I went to Spain for a few days before I flew from there to Italy and did a foodie tour from Milan to Parma, Modena and Bologna. I told myself I was carb loading for the baby and I went all in on every type of pasta I could get my hands on, what better excuse than eating for two? It got a bit out of hand to be honest and I could barely roll myself out of the restaurants at the end.

As a side note, the Italians I encountered throughout this trip were brilliant. When they noticed I was pregnant they would go above and beyond to make sure I was comfortable and looked after everywhere I went. I found it mortifying but very sweet.

After that trip, I had one last hurrah and went over to Spain with my Stepmum, Suzy, and we had a relaxing few days in the sunshine and I was into the eighth month of the world's longest pregnancy at this point so I was probably pushing the limits. Suzy was extremely concerned I might go into labour on the trip and was telling me she was not emotionally equipped to be a birthing partner on such short notice. Luckily for us all everything was fine, and we returned home as two ticketed passengers, not three.

A month later Evelyn was born.

Chapter 3

WTF do we do now?

Evelyn arrived via C-section at exactly 39 weeks, healthy, perfect and with a full head of dark hair. And, judging by the expression on her face when she was presented to me like Simba on Pride Rock, she was livid about it.

That first night in the hospital was certainly an experience. Mike went off home to have a 'proper' sleep whilst Evelyn and I were melting on the hottest hospital ward I've ever experienced. I also discovered when I returned to the ward with Evelyn, that the posh M&S sandwiches my Mum had kindly brought for me, had all been scoffed by Mike whilst I was in recovery. He was not top of my friends list that day. Once my rage had subsided and I could see clearly again without the red mist, I stared down at this tiny little bundle of black hair wrapped in her blankets and had one singular thought… 'you're adorable but WTF do we do now?'.

I was still immobile at this stage, numb from the ribs down and unable to sit up. So, whenever Evelyn needed something, I had to use the buzzer to call for one of the lovely nurses to come and help us. They were incredible and I am very grateful they managed to source me some food after sandwich-gate. However, the next morning, having been far too hot to get any meaningful sleep, I was very keen to be discharged and sent on my way.

I still it find it extremely alarming that not even 24 hours after delivering your baby, your **first** baby, the nurses happily pack you up and send you off into the world. Somehow, they are confident that you are magically equipped with the knowledge and skills to keep this fragile little person safe and well until adulthood. Maybe they think we've read all the books and are raring to go. We hadn't. We were freestyling. I vividly remember packing my bags and thinking 'are they sure we can just leave? Don't we have to pass some sort of test? How are we going to know what to do?!'. But off we went, the epitome of all the gear and no idea with Evelyn packed into her car seat, looking just as shell shocked as we were.

When we got back home with our new arrival, we decided to go straight out for a walk to get some fresh air and some caffeine. God knows we needed it. We wanted a bit of normality after being stuck in the hospital, so we took Evelyn for her first trip to Costa. People were staring at us like we were mad because we'd put her in her baby carrier not realising that there was a minimum height requirement, and she was definitely too small for it at 2 days old. All you could see were two tiny legs poking out.

Apart from our exciting trip to Costa, that first week as a family of three was a total blur of visitors, pink balloons and more adorable outfits than Evelyn could ever wear. I was sustained almost entirely by Dominos pizzas and coffee. Carb loading was my personality at this stage. The only strong memory that I have from this bizarre period of fatigue and newborn baby chaos, is that when my Dad first came to meet Evelyn with my little sister Tilly, he decided to whip his t-shirt off without warning and announce to us all that he got his nipple pierced. I can only assume he was having some sort of crisis about becoming a Grandad at 52 but it stopped us all in our tracks for a good few minutes. Welcome to the world, Evelyn. This is your Grandad. This type of behaviour will likely continue for your whole life I'm afraid and I can only apologise.

Before Evelyn arrived, Mike and I had several discussions about how we wanted to spend those first few months and how we could make the most of them to spend time together as a three. I am fortunate enough to work remotely and Mike works unpredictable hours for the NHS, so with that in mind we decided to split the entitlement between us.

In the end I took just 6 weeks off work and Mike took 6 months off from his job. This was great and allowed him to have longer with our new baby instead of the usual 2 weeks he would have been able to take otherwise, and this was invaluable to us in the early days. Whilst I appreciate that this is not an option for everybody and depends on your individual circumstances, for us it made sense, and we were able to make it work. It was time that we certainly made the most of as you will see in this book and, even if we hadn't used that time to travel so much, it would have been amazing just to have Mike at home to spend time with Evelyn and to help me out.

Once we had organised how much leave we were taking and knowing that we would now have so much time together as a new family, we were wondering how to spend it. I tentatively suggested that it might be nice to go on a little holiday during our parental leave to catch our breath and allow us to spend time just us three without the revolving door of visitors we knew we would have.

Everybody that I spoke to about our plans to go abroad with our newborn baby was either horrified or very surprised. But what if the baby gets sick? The baby won't have had her injections. What if you're really tired and she doesn't sleep well? What if you get stranded there? How will you cope away from family? How will you get her there? All valid questions, albeit not always anybody's business, but the overall reaction of shock and disapproval was quite surprising to me at the time. I am the type of person who likes to push boundaries and do difficult things. I like the challenge of doing something that I am told I cannot possibly do.

Naturally, experiencing this reaction from people only served to make me more determined for us to go out into the world and try not to let the anxieties and doubts of others cast gloomy clouds over my hopeful plans. One of my concerns was that, if I let the fears of others start affecting my decisions about going abroad or going anywhere else for that matter, then that fear might start to grow legs. I might get to the point where I didn't want to take Evelyn anywhere at all, I might stay in my house and it could escalate into a bigger issue than it was. I had no idea how I was going to feel when I became a mother so all I could do was do what I felt was right for us at the time. With this in mind, we started planning.

When we first talked about the idea of taking Evelyn abroad, we couldn't decide where to go or how long to go away for and tensions were high due to all the anxiety that comes with having a newborn baby. What if we **are** stranded somewhere and she needs medical assistance? What if we **can't** get back? What if we **can't** fit all the stuff on the plane that we need to take? What if this country runs completely out of nappies and baby wipes and we are forced to improvise?!

What was originally going to be a trip to Mallorca, somewhere with a short flight, a family apartment close to the airport and good hospitals and amenities, quickly evolved into a month-long trip to France. This is the way things often work out when I am planning a trip and I struggle to just 'keep it simple'.

After a lot of discussions, a few irrational thoughts and a couple hours of Googling, we decided that we would drive to France and take our own car, with our own things to make sure we had everything we thought we would need. **Spoiler alert**: we went overboard. The car was so heavy that there were more than a couple of dodgy moments where I didn't think we'd make it up the hills.

Once we had decided we would be spending a month in France with our newborn, I had to consider the logistics of getting a baby and all her things to France. No easy task. Now, as I was having an elective C-section I roughly knew the date of Evelyn's birth and I booked an appointment to register her birth for 2 weeks after my C-section date as, at that time, it was quite difficult to get appointments. I also booked an appointment at the passport office for the same week.

Fortuitously, everything went to plan, and we went to register Evelyn's birth as planned. After a last-minute panic about whether it was cruel to give a child the initials ELF, we had her birth certificate in hand. Step 2 complete. Now it was onto the next big appointment, The Passport Office. Oddly, I was not required to present Evelyn in person, they just took my word for it, a couple of forms and her birth certificate. The passport came a week later.

The passport photo that we ended up with is truly terrible. At two weeks old she was lying on an enormous white sheet in the middle of Timpsons whilst a heavily muscled, tattooed man took her photograph. She will have that passport now until she is 5 years old and every time I present it at border control I am convinced someone will accuse me of trying to traffic a child. They should probably look at that 5-year rule as in a lot of other countries the passport is only valid for 2 years and I expect it is for that very reason.

Once we decided to make the journey to France by car, we drove down to London first and we visited some friends and family who hadn't met Evelyn yet. For some reason Mike had agreed to volunteer as a medic at the London Marathon which was happening in October that year, so Evelyn and I cheered on a couple of friends at the halfway point on Tower Bridge. We took Evelyn to Flight Club in London that night for reasons that remain unknown. My friend Emily and I were trying to get inside and security told us that they couldn't allow me in with somebody underage. After Emily assured them that we'd keep Evelyn off the g&t's we were finally allowed in for our final night in the UK before our big adventure.

The next morning, bright eyed and bushy tailed we drove down to Southampton for the next leg of our journey as we were going over to France on the ferry from there.

So, at 4 weeks old with a new passport and her new coat on; a very unimpressed Evelyn was bundled onto the ferry and was on her way to France for a month.

Chapter 4

The Benefits of Traveling with Your Baby

Traveling with a baby might seem daunting at first, but there are so many benefits for both the parent and the child. This chapter explores the ways in which travel, and these new experiences can positively influence a baby's development.

As you'll see throughout the pages of this book, there have been a few moments on our adventures where things have been chaotic, stressful and haven't necessarily gone to plan. When I recounted these stories to friends and family, a common question I was asked was 'was it worth it?'. At times I have questioned myself when things have been difficult. Is it worth it? When it comes down to it, the answer for me is yes. It is always worth it and the benefits of travel will always outweigh the difficult moments.

All babies are naturally curious, and they are constantly learning about the world through their senses. Every new environment is a sensory adventure for our little explorers. By travelling with them, you are exposing them to a range of different sensory experiences – including new sights, smells, tastes and textures. They can experience the vibrant colours and exciting sounds of a busy city and feel the waves lapping against their little toes in the sea. The variety of stimuli you encounter will enhance your baby's development and expose them to a diverse, exciting new environment.

The progress that Evelyn has made in both her confidence and her speech and language development over the past 12 months has been brilliant. She has developed such a curiosity about the world and other people. She has learnt to say 'hello' in 4 languages and can say 'thank you' in a couple more. Through exposure to different cultures, different places and different people she is a very confident, happy little girl.

Travelling isn't always smooth sailing – there are detours, delays, and unexpected surprises around every corner. But through all these experiences your baby is learning to roll with the punches. They're adapting to new situations and handling whatever comes their way. Adaptability is an important life skill to learn.

Every new experience helps your baby build confidence. They're learning that they can tackle new challenges and explore the big wide world around them. Every adventure is giving them a confidence boost and a chance to develop new skills.

One of the best parts of travelling for me is the opportunity to try new foods. From spicy curries to seafood paellas, your baby can experience so many new tastes and textures. There's evidence that exposing little ones to a variety of flavours early on can make them less fussy eaters in the long run and I am sure that this can only be a good thing.

As soon as we started weaning Evelyn off milk and onto solids at 5 months old, we gave her whatever we were eating in whichever country we were in at the time. We flirted with the idea of jars of baby food briefly, but she made her distaste for that idea quite clear. She was as keen on the prospect of eating green mush as you or I would be. We didn't bother after that and just let her eat whatever we ate. Nowadays she loves paella, olives, chorizo, goulash, trofie al pesto (who doesn't?) and everything in between. She will give everything a try and for the most part will demolish whatever you put in front of her, at an alarming speed.

I appreciate that this won't be the same for every baby and we are fortunate that Evelyn is a) relatively easy-going and b) doesn't appear to have any intolerances thus far. As I am quite lazy in the culinary department, I am thrilled that I don't have to make separate meals for us all. As Evelyn will eat anything it does make eating out abroad (and at home) slightly less complicated.

Because of the trips that we've been on, Evelyn is used to different modes of transport and doesn't worry about going on boats, planes, trains, gondolas or cable cars. When she was a month old, we took her into some huge caves in Gouffre de Padirac, where we were taken on a tiny boat deep in the caves in the dark with bats flying around our heads. We hadn't realised that's what the trip would entail when we bought our tickets, but Evelyn took it in her stride.

I am extremely proud of how Evelyn has developed and the adventures that we have had so far have been such a lovely bonding experience for us as a three.

Whilst we have taken many trips together as a family of three, I have also done my fair share of travelling with Evelyn on my own. I took her to Austria then across into Slovakia by coach, into Slovenia and then finished in Budapest, Hungary. That trip was a big test for me and how I would deal with not just taking Evelyn abroad alone, but to navigate us across 4 countries. It was a great experience, and I am proud of myself for doing it.

It was nice to spend so much time with Evelyn just the two of us and it was incredible to watch her exploring new places. She'd just begun to walk when I took her on that trip and she spent a lot of time pottering around in parks getting to grips with her new walking skills.

Chapter 5

Shared Parental Leave

When I tell people how much travelling we did with Evelyn in her first 6 months, I am often asked: how did we manage it? How did Mike get so much time off? The answer is that we took shared parental leave, a concept that seems to be used infrequently in the UK compared to traditional leave.

Shared Parental Leave (SPL) represents a significant evolution in the landscape of family-friendly policies in the United Kingdom. It was introduced to promote gender equality and provide families with greater flexibility, SPL allows parents to share leave in the first year following the birth or adoption of their child. This chapter delves into the specifics of SPL, including its legislative framework, eligibility criteria, benefits, and the broader implications for families and employers.

Framework

The concept of SPL was introduced through the Children and Families Act 2014, coming into effect in April 2015. This act amended previous maternity, paternity, and adoption leave regulations, establishing a more inclusive approach to parental responsibilities. The SPL regulations are designed to complement existing maternity leave laws, allowing both parents to participate more equally in the early stages of their child's life.

Under these regulations, SPL allows eligible parents to share up to 50 weeks of leave and 37 weeks of pay. This is part of the total 52 weeks of maternity leave, with the first two weeks after birth reserved exclusively for the mother.

Eligibility

The eligibility for SPL is based on several criteria, ensuring that both the employee and their partner meet specific conditions:

1. Employment Status:

(a) both parents must be employed

(b) one parent must have worked for the employers for at least 26 weeks by the end of the 15th week before the due date (or adoption date).

(c) the other parent must have worked (either as an employee or self-employed) for at least 26 weeks in the 66 weeks leading up to the due date, earning a minimum of £30 per week for 13 of those weeks.

2. Maternity Leave and Pay

(a) the mother must end her maternity leave or pay early, converting the remaining entitlement into SPL.

(b) for adoption, the primary adopter must end their adoption leave of pay early.

3. Notification and Planning

(a) parents must notify their employers at least eight weeks in advance of their intention to take SPL but, of course, the sooner you notify them the better. Particularly if they aren't used to processing SPL requests as the administration can be cumbersome.

(b) a 'notice of entitlement and intention' form must be submitted outlining how the leave will be shared.

(c) the employer can request evidence of the partner's employment income.

4. Benefits and Pay

Shared Parental Pay (ShPP) is available for up to 37 weeks. The rate of ShPP is set by the government and is reviewed annually. As of the 2023/24 tax year, ShPP is the lower of £172.48 per week or 90% of the employee's average weekly earnings.

Parents can take SPL in continuous blocks or multiple discontinuous blocks, providing greater flexibility. This flexibility allows parents to stagger their leave or even take it simultaneously, depending on their family's needs. We took our simultaneously to allow us all to travel together.

Practical Implications for Families

The introduction of SPL has several significant implications for families:

1. Gender Equality:

SPL encourages a more balanced approach to childcare responsibilities, challenging traditional gender roles. Fathers and partners are given more opportunities to bond with their child and participate in caregiving.

2. Flexibility:

Families can tailor their leave arrangements to better suit their personal and professional circumstances and this flexibility can reduce the financial and career impact of taking time off work. This is one of the reasons that I returned to work sooner.

3. Work Life Balance

SPL can improve the work-life balance for both parents, contributing to better mental health and well-being. It also allows parents to manage their return to work more gradually, easing the transition.

Challenges and Criticisms

Despite its benefits, SPL faces several challenges:

1. Low Uptake

The initial uptake of SPL has been lower than anticipated, attributed to cultural norms, financial concerns and general lack of awareness.

Many fathers remain reluctant to take SPL due to fears of negative career impacts.

2. Complexity

The process of applying for and managing SPL can be complex, requiring detailed coordination between parents and employers.

3. Financial Constraints

For many families, the financial aspect of ShPP, which is lower than the typical salary, can be a deterrent and higher-earning families may find the reduced income difficult to manage during SPL.

Overall, Shared Parental Leave represents a progressive step towards greater gender equality and flexibility for families in the UK. While the policy has its challenges, its potential to reshape family dynamics and workplace culture is significant. With continued efforts to raise awareness, simplify the process, and address financial concerns, SPL can become a more widely utilized and impactful provision for parents across the country. As society evolves, so too must the policies that support families, ensuring that both parents have the opportunity to participate fully in their child's early life without undue hardship.

Without SPL, we would not have been able to travel as much as we did in those first 6 months of Evelyn's life.

Chapter 6

12 Countries in 12 months

By Evelyn's first birthday, as well as hitting all the usual developmental milestones, she achieved something quite unusual for somebody so small. She visited 12 countries in those first 12 months of her life.

Many of these countries will be talked about throughout the pages of this book, we covered a lot of ground in those first 12 months, and we had an incredible experience in (almost!) every place. We found that as we did each new trip it got easier to pack, to get around and we felt more relaxed going abroad. However, just as the logistics got easier, Evelyn got older, more mobile and more challenging (I say that with love, of course).

The past 12 months travelling have taught me so much about myself and my parenting style. The experience itself and the challenges that we have faced along the way have reshaped my values, strategies, and perspectives as a parent. This chapter explores the ways in which traveling has changed my parenting style from how I was on day 1 to how I am today.

1. Embracing Flexibility

    Travelling, especially with a baby, demands a high level of flexibility. Plans often change due to unforeseen circumstances like weather, health issues, or unexpected opportunities. This need for adaptability has significantly influenced my parenting style. I've learned to be more flexible and to adjust our routines and expectations based on my baby's needs and the environment we're in. This adaptability has made me more patient and open-minded.

2. Prioritising Experiences Over Possessions

The past 12 months have shown me the value of experiences over material possessions. The memories and lessons gained from exploring new places, meeting different people, and engaging in various activities are far more beneficial than any physical object. This realisation has shifted my focus as a parent towards creating meaningful experiences for my child. I prioritise activities that promote learning, exploration, and bonding, rather than buying Evelyn more toys and gadgets that she'll quickly tire of.

3. Encouraging Independence and Confidence

Travelling often involves navigating unfamiliar environments and facing new challenges. These experiences have encouraged me to encourage independence and confidence in my child. I've learned to give my baby the space to explore, make choices, and learn from new experiences, even at this young age. This encouragement of autonomy has helped build my child's confidence and problem-solving skills. It has also taught me to trust in my child's abilities and to try to be less overprotective. My heart is still in my mouth at least 10 times a day when I watch her jumping, running and climbing on things, but we're getting there.

4. Enhancing Problem Solving Skills

The unpredictable nature of travel requires constant problem-solving and quick thinking. Whether it's finding alternative routes, managing travel logistics, or dealing with huge problems, these situations have honed my problem-solving skills. This ability to think on my feet has translated into my parenting style, making me more resourceful and resilient when dealing with the curveballs life throws my way.

5. Cultivating Patience and Presence

Going travelling with a baby requires a great deal of patience and presence. Delays, disruptions, and the temperament of my baby have taught me to slow down and be more present in the moment. I've learned to appreciate the small moments more and to listen more attentively. I try not to go into everything 100 miles an hour, which is my usual approach to most facets of my life.

6. Valuing Quality Time

The time spent with Mike and Evelyn during these trips, particularly in the first 6 months of Evelyn's life have shown the importance of quality time together. During the usual day to day stresses of work, appointments and social engagements it can be difficult to prioritise time in the same way.

7. Building a Resilient and Positive Mindset

The ups and downs of travel have fostered resilience and a positive mindset in both me and my child. Overcoming challenges and embracing new experiences with a positive attitude has become a central part of our approach to life. As a parent, I try to demonstrate resilience and optimism, which I hope will encourage my child to view challenges as opportunities for growth and learning as she gets older.

My approach to most things is not to worry too much, it'll all work out itself out in the end which is a good mindset to have when you have a little bundle of chaos.

8. Lessons Learned

In hindsight, I wish that we had been a bit more daring within those first few months and had gone further afield. What I didn't appreciate when Evelyn was a newborn baby, is how much easier it is to ferry babies around when they are unable to walk or crawl. Things get much more difficult when they can hop off your knee and run down the aisle of the plane trying to pinch people's crisps. However, I am proud of us for taking the plunge and taking Evelyn abroad at all at 4 weeks old as it started this journey and led to this book being written.

Chapter 7

Baby Friendly Destinations

The first step in planning a trip with your little one is deciding where to go. Choosing a baby-friendly destination can make all the difference in helping create a holiday to remember.

What kind of trip are you looking for? An all-inclusive hotel where you don't have to leave the resort? A city hopping trip around Europe? A beachfront apartment in Thailand? Something in between?

Here are some factors to consider and a few recommendations for you:

Factors to Consider:

<u>1. Climate:</u>

When planning your trip, you need to consider the weather at your destination. We all know babies can be sensitive to extreme temperatures, so the ideal weather would be mild and comfortable climates where possible. It's best to avoid very hot or very cold locations if possible, and always check the seasonal weather forecasts at your chosen destination to avoid any surprises. I did not do this on our first trip.

When we took Evelyn to France in October, she was a month old, and we expected autumnal weather and colder temperatures. That's what I had packed for after doing my research. I'd taken three snowsuits. When we got there it was an average of 25 degrees and sunny the whole 4 weeks we were there. I had packed a hadn't packed any suncream. First parenting fail - tick.

2. Healthcare:

It is advisable to research the healthcare facilities available at your destination. It can alleviate anxieties and be reassuring to know that quality medical care is accessible in the unlikely case of any emergencies. Look for destinations with reputable hospitals and clinics, especially if you're traveling to a developing country.

When we took Evelyn to Egypt and she required urgent hospital treatment we hadn't done this research before we went and had to rely on Google and Mike's colleague who was from Cairo, where we were staying, to recommend a hospital to us. Google gives hospitals in Egypt ratings out of 5 stars, like you're selecting a hotel. It was a very interesting experience, so I always recommend doing your research in advance to avoid a scenario like ours.

The hospital we went to was brilliant and they saw Evelyn within 15 minutes and treated her immediately. We were sent on our way with a bag full of antibiotics within the hour and it only cost £13 in total. They take your credit card off you when you enter the hospital along with your ID and I couldn't do the conversion of Egyptian pounds very well, so I had no idea how much we were paying until it came through on our bank statement. A very good expenditure of money and Evelyn was right as rain within 24 hours.

3. Safety:

It goes without saying that safety is a top priority when traveling with a baby. Check travel advisories and read up on the safety of your chosen destination. Look for family-friendly places with low crime rates and a welcoming atmosphere for tourists. Ensure that the reviews you are reading are current. Some reviews can show at the top for a destination, but they are over 10 years old, and the information can be out of date.

4. Accessibility:

Another consideration when choosing a location for you and your baby is accessibility. You will want to choose destinations that are easy to navigate with a baby. Look out for places with good infrastructure, including pram-friendly pavements, accessible public transportation, and baby-friendly accommodations. If you're planning on attending cultural sites and experiences, you may also want to check their policies on allowing prams inside and what baby changing facilities they may offer.

It is my recommendation to take a baby carrier when travelling anywhere. It is useful to take the pram for when your baby is older and finds it more difficult to nap in a carrier and for parking them whilst you have a coffee or something to eat but a baby carrier is always my preference. In crowded places or places with a lot of steps or cobbles, a pram can be cumbersome whereas you can move around easily with the carrier and it allows you to be hands-free.

5. Amenities:

When selecting a destination, you need to consider the availability of baby essentials such as nappies, formula, and baby food. While it is possible to pack most items to take with you, the knowledge that you can easily find what you need at your destination can reduce stress at the airport. This can allow you to carry less luggage which can be particularly important if you are travelling alone with your baby and are unable to carry multiple bags as well as your baby. The struggle of carrying everything, plus your baby and trying to wrestle passports out of compartments can be stressful.

Top Recommended Destinations:

1. **Rome, Italy**

    Why it's Great: History around every corner and beautiful piazzas to explore. Italian love for children makes it a very welcoming place.

    Family Perks: Delicious food, accommodating restaurants, and plenty of open spaces to enjoy.

    I'd recommend anywhere in Italy to be honest; it's been our absolute favourite place to go with Evelyn and we've been back several times. It's a fantastic place to take a baby.

2. **Lisbon, Portugal**

    Why it's Great: Charming, colourful streets and a welcoming atmosphere. The weather is usually great, and there are many scenic spots to sit and relax. There is so much to do and the food is incredible.

    Family Perks: There is a lot to see and do and locals are very welcoming to families with babies.

3. **Barcelona, Spain**

   <u>Why it's Great</u>: Warm weather and beach access make it a lovely spot for sun and relaxation but there's no shortage of things to see or do. The architecture is incredible. The wide, tree-lined streets are great for walking with a pram.

   <u>Family Perks</u>: Abundant parks and playgrounds, plus delicious food and tapas culture. Siestas are a big plus.

4. **Athens, Greece:**

   <u>Why it's Great:</u> it is rich in history and culture with plenty of open-air spaces like the National Gardens and the Acropolis. It has beautiful seaside promenades and boat trips available to the neighbouring islands.

   <u>Family Perks:</u> Greek people are so friendly and seem to love children. We found a lot of helping hands ready to assist us at any time. The warm weather is great for outdoor activities with your baby and the food is incredible.

5. **Palma, Mallorca**

   <u>Why it's Great:</u> Stunning beaches and an incredible old town. Lots for your baby to see and do. The food is delicious.

   <u>Family Perks:</u> The island is very small, so you are able to do a lot of exploring with your baby without hours of travel time. Restaurants and cafés are very baby friendly, and the island is mostly pram-friendly.

6. **Amsterdam, Netherlands**

   Why It's Great: Flat terrain makes it super pram-friendly, and the canals provide beautiful scenery. Plus, there are plenty of parks like Vondelpark where you can relax and let your baby explore.

   Family Perks: Excellent public transportation and baby-friendly cafés everywhere.

7. **Paris, France**

   Why it's Great: Iconic landmarks, beautiful gardens like Luxembourg Gardens, lots to see and do. Lots of delicious pastries and foods available. Taking a boat trip on the Seine is incredible with a baby.

   Family Perks: Plenty of parks, excellent public transport, and lots of cafés to relax in.

   I would usually put this higher on the list as it's one of my favourite cities of all time, but it is quite difficult to navigate the cobbled streets with a pram and some parts of Paris have a lot of steps, so accessibility is not the best compared to these other locations.

8. **Vienna, Austria**

   Why it's Great: Beautiful and calm, and full of gardens to explore like Schönbrunn Palace's grounds where you can enjoy peaceful walks and let your baby roam.

   Family Perks: Lots of baby-friendly facilities and easy navigation through the city.

9. **Dubrovnik, Croatia**

Why it's Great: It has stunning coastal views and a historic town and crystal-clear waters. The old town is perfect for talking walks with your baby.

Family Perks: Pram-friendly and lots of friendly locals. Very safe and lots of baby-friendly restaurants to try.

10. **Kotor, Montenegro**

Why it's Great: Kotor offers stunning mountain and sea views as well as a medieval old town. It is perfect for a relaxing trip with your baby.

Family Perks: The town is small and easy to navigate with a pram. It is baby friendly and has lots of restaurants and bars. It is the ideal place for taking a stroll and enjoying a slow paced holiday.

Europe in particular is full of amazing destinations that cater to families with young children. These cities offer fantastic amenities, welcoming locals, and plenty of beautiful, relaxing spots for you and your little one to enjoy.

We have been to some places that are further afield, but they didn't quite make my top 10 list!

Chapter 8

Preparing for the Journey: Packing

Once you've chosen your destination, it's time to start doing some planning and, the worst part of any trip, packing. This chapter is intended to give you some tips and information about what may be helpful to you when travelling with your baby. Anything essential that you find you have forgotten or have run out of, you can pick up when you arrive – so don't worry too much if you leave something behind.

As eager new parents, who bought everything the internet told us to during my pregnancy (what a mistake), we packed our car to the point of bursting for our first trip. A few of the 'essentials' I brought with me were: my Tommee Tippee prep machine, 20 bottles, a huge microwave steriliser, a full changing mat, our huge pram, multiple tins of formula, so many nappies, 40 onesies (no really), a baby wetsuit (don't) and a baby rocker. The only reason I didn't take the baby bath is because the boot wouldn't close. I bathed her in the sink without a fancy little hammock, like the olden days, and she lived to tell the tale.

Needless to say, I took so many things that we really did not need and, on our next trip abroad, I took less than half of what I'd packed for France. I have sought to give you a list below of what you might need depending on how long you're going for and what might work for your baby. This is a comprehensive list so you may find you only take a few things from it, we often only take a few of these items, especially as we got more confident travelling and as Evelyn got a bit older.

Comprehensive Packing List for Baby Essentials:

Nappies & Wipes

I'll say this from the outset, you do not need necessarily need to bring a whole multipack of nappies with you. If you can fit them in your case and it's easy enough to bring them, do it. If you're travelling light with hand luggage only, I recommend that you bring enough for the first day or two and purchase some when you arrive in your destination. This is going to depend on where you're travelling to and how accessible shops are to your accommodation.

Usually, we stay in apartments or hotels in major cities or towns and there is usually a Carrefour or Lidl or equivalent or a corner shop somewhere nearby where you can source nappies and wipes. This can greatly reduce the amount of luggage you have to take with you an alleviate stress at the airport, particularly if you are on your own.

I'm not sure what my thought process was when I went to France on that first trip, but I was clearly in the mindset of a Doomsday prepper. I stockpiled nappies and formula and, in my post-partum haze, I appeared to have forgotten that they have supermarkets in France. I learnt from this mistake very quickly and now only tend to pack a handful of nappies to take with us and I buy a pack when we arrive at our destination.

If you do want to take nappies and wipes for the entirety of your trip, a good rule of thumb is to how many nappies you'll likely need for the duration of your trip and pack an extra one for each day. I've had situations where I have packed exactly enough for a couple of days and then have unexpectedly gone through 4 nappies in the airport alone.

Don't forget to pack plenty of wipes for quick clean-ups, usually I take 3 packets with me and always end up buying another packet at my destination no matter how long I'm going for. Especially when your little one starts weaning and everything, and everyone, is suddenly orange.

Clothing:

Layering is key, especially if you're traveling to a place with variable weather (anywhere in Europe pretty much!). You want to be packing snowsuits, hats, mittens or a sunhat if necessary. I have tried to get Evelyn to wear sunglasses many times but have never had much success, so I don't bother now. I always have a couple of spare outfits handy in my plane bag and have called upon them many a time after poo explosions in the airport where the original outfit had to be binned.

Feeding Supplies:

If you're breastfeeding, bring any necessary pumps or storage bags that you may use. For formula-fed babies, pack enough formula, bottles, and a portable sterilizer if needed. Don't overdo it on the bottles like I did. You only really need 5 max. if you can sterilise and clean them where you're staying. Save yourself the space.

Evelyn was formula-fed, and it did greatly increase the amount of luggage we had, as I took our prep machine on most trips when she was mostly drinking milk. As she got a bit older, I opted for a portable formula maker as we were making bottles less frequently.

Don't forget snacks and baby food for older infants, particularly for your plane bag – I've made this mistake before. Nobody on the plane thanked me for it as Evelyn howled from when we landed until we were past the passport queue.

Sleep Essentials:

For sleeping, you should bring your baby's sleep sack and blanket and a portable crib or travel cot if you use them. If your baby relies on a white noise machine to get to sleep, you can get small travel size ones to take with you which can save luggage space. I always pack a couple of books for bedtime and a cuddly toy. Familiar items can help your baby sleep better in unfamiliar surroundings if they struggle to get to sleep outside of their usual environment.

As we usually opt for apartments, I tend to book ones that have a cot included to save bringing ours with us. We have had a few situations where the travel cot wasn't actually in our apartment when we arrived and, in those instances, we have co-slept and have not had any issues. I appreciate not everybody will be comfortable doing that so if you are worried, I would recommend that you do bring a travel cot. The one we have is essentially a tiny pop-up tent with a self-inflating mattress and it is suitable for babies and lasts them up to the age of 3. My brother is 6'2 and managed to fold himself up to fit inside Evelyn's so they do last a while!

First Aid Kit:

If you want to make sure you are super prepared for all eventualities, then you can take a first aid kit with you. This should include baby-specific items such as infant pain reliever, teething gel, and any prescription medications. A thermometer and basic first-aid supplies are also useful additions.

Again, try not to worry about packing absolutely everything because the likelihood is you will be able to access a pharmacy to acquire any other items your baby may need. We don't usually pack a first aid kit but I've lost count of the number of times we've been in a pharmacy abroad buying their equivalent of Calpol, we usually remember the syringe but forget the Calpol. Make sure you also pack suncream if you're going somewhere with a bit of sunshine.

Baby Gear:

I recommend that you take a lightweight pram (ideally one that folds up quite small), a baby carrier, and a portable highchair if your baby is old enough. These items can make your travels much easier. Anything that is compact and easy to fold or pack is your best friend.

One item we could have easily done without during our time in France, was the pram. I was very excited to debut our Brand New Pram so I forced it into the boot of our car and it took up the majority of boot space. We used it twice. We used our baby carrier pretty much exclusively the whole time we were away. If we weren't using the baby carrier, we carried her or sat her on our knees. This was not a travel pram - it was huge. In hindsight, I should have left it behind and bought a travel pram instead, particularly because a lot of the places we visited in France were not pram friendly anyway.

My Mum bought us a travel pram which we used for all of our other adventures, and it was a lifesaver. The one we have folds up small enough to fit in a tote bag so it's easy to take on the plane with us and put in the overhead locker. The only problem we have with it, is that it does not lie down flat so, now that Evelyn is older, she struggles to nap in it. I would recommend a travel pram that can lie flat.

Toys and Teddies:

Pack a few of your baby's favourite toys and teddies to keep them entertained and calm during the trip. I have recently bought Evelyn a 'busy book' and it keeps her entertained for a long time as she tries to fasten and unfasten the various clips. Be careful with these because Amazon have recalled a couple in recent months due to safety concerns as some of them have some small pieces.

Tips for Efficient Packing and Minimizing Stress:

Make a List:

I love a list. Start with a comprehensive packing list to ensure you don't forget anything important. Check off items as you pack them to stay organised and avoid that last minute 'I've forgotten the formula' panic on the way to the airport.

Pack in Advance:

I should practice what I preach here but try to avoid last-minute stress by packing a few days before your departure. This gives you time to add any forgotten items and reduces pre-travel anxieties. Check your list!

Use Packing Cubes:

Packing cubes can help you stay really organised and maximize space in your luggage. You can use them to separate baby's items from your own as well as separating clean and dirty things during your trip.

Carry-On Essentials:

Pack a small carry-on bag with all the essentials you'll need during the flight or travel time, such as nappies, wipes, a changing mat, a change of clothes, snacks, drinks and toys.

I would also recommend that you pack a change of clothes for you as well. On a recent trip to Spain, Evelyn managed to get poo out of the side of her nappy, out of her dress and onto my lap and shoes. This was whilst we were in the middle of our flight, so I had to carry her down the aisle like an active grenade and change her. I did not have any clothes for me in my plane bag and had to sit there with remnants of poo on my leg until I got off the plane - 0/10 would not recommend.

Baby Food & Milk in Carry-On:

If you are taking any bottles of milk, either in your baby's bottle or the sealed travel milks, they will need to come out of your hand luggage at security and go into a separate tray.

This is the same for formula and any wet baby food. It doesn't have to be put in a liquids bag; but it will need to be in a separate tray to the rest of your liquids and other items. Try to keep it separately in your hand luggage to make it easier to separate when you get to security; it's a nightmare having people tutting behind you as you try and dig to the bottom of your bag for a stray jar of baby food.

Liquids:

The rules on liquids allowed in your carry-on are changing in June 2024 to allow you to carry on larger volume liquids in your hand luggage. This will be particularly useful when taking suncream and the like for babies.

Keep Important Documents and Money Handy:

Store your passports, travel insurance, car hire documents, driving licences, other important documents and money in an easily accessible place. Consider a travel wallet or organiser for added convenience. Ours is hot pink and covered in sequins and Mike hates it. I probably need to buy something a little more lowkey.

Travel Documents and Legalities:

Before you embark on your adventure, ensure that all necessary travel documents are in order. This includes:

Passports and Visas:

Make sure your baby has a valid passport and check the visa requirements for your destination. Some countries may have specific entry requirements for infants.

Health and Travel Insurance:

I do recommend that you purchase comprehensive travel insurance that covers your baby. Check that it includes coverage for medical emergencies, trip cancellations, and lost luggage. This is a very important one and one that I almost forgot to do before we went on our trip to Greece and Egypt and that was the trip where we ended up in the hospital.

A lot of banks provide travel insurance with current accounts now but we always purchase a higher level of cover for Evelyn separately when we go away just in case.

<u>Immunisation Records:</u>

Depending on where you're travelling to, you may need to carry a copy of your baby's immunisation records. Some countries may require proof of certain vaccinations upon entry. Always check the requirements of your travel destination before you set off to ensure you have everything that you and your baby will need.

Chapter 9

Health & Safety

Pre-Travel Health Preparations

Here she is, Captain Sensible: one of the most important aspects of travelling with a baby is ensuring their health and safety. If you're a first-time parent, the idea of taking your baby somewhere new might seem a bit daunting.

Here she is, Little Miss Lawyer: please note that I am not a doctor, and the information given below is not health advice. You should always consult your health professional for specific advice.

Vaccinations and Immunisations

I know this can be controversial, but if there's some medication you can give to your child to keep them safe from wholly preventable illnesses then it's a good idea to have them before taking them on holiday. If you're taking your baby away before their first vaccinations are due then this section will not apply to you but keep it in mind for future trips.

The NHS vaccination schedule covers a range of important immunisations, and staying on track with these is vital. Here's a quick rundown of what to keep in mind:

1. <u>Consult with Your GP</u>

If in doubt, schedule an appointment with your GP to discuss your travel plans. They can advise on any additional vaccinations that may be recommended based on your destination. For example, some countries may require vaccines for diseases not commonly found in the UK, such as Hepatitis A or B, and in rare cases, yellow fever.

2. <u>Carry Vaccination Records</u>

It is generally recommended that you bring a copy of your baby's vaccination records. Some countries may require proof of certain immunisations upon entry. It's a good idea to keep a digital copy on your phone as well, just in case.

Consulting with Paediatricians

Your baby's GP or paediatrician is a valuable resource when planning travel. They can provide specific advice tailored to both your baby's health needs and your travel itinerary.

Health Check-Up

If you feel that it would benefit you and your baby, you can arrange for a check-up to ensure your baby is in good health before you travel.

Medications and Prescriptions

If your baby is on any medication, make sure you have enough to last the entire trip, plus a little extra in case of delays. Ask your GP for a prescription you can carry with you and get a doctor's note explaining any necessary medications.

Managing Health Abroad

Being prepared for health issues that might arise while you're travelling can give you peace of mind and ease the anxiety of the 'what ifs'. Here are some tips on how to handle medical care abroad:

Finding and Accessing Medical Care:

Research Healthcare Facilities:

Before you travel, you can research the healthcare facilities available at your destination. It can help ease worry if you identify the nearest hospitals, clinics, and pharmacies. Websites like the NHS's Fit for Travel offer comprehensive advice on healthcare resources in various countries.

Travel Insurance:

Ensure you have comprehensive travel insurance that covers medical expenses for your baby. This is non-negotiable for me; medical care abroad can be very costly without it. Check that your policy includes everything that you need it to.

Emergency Contacts:

Keep a list of emergency contacts handy, including local emergency services, your embassy, and your travel insurance provider's number. If you are partial to trying a new language it can also be helpful to learn a few key phrases in the local language related to health and emergencies.

My best friend, Becki, is always keen to show off her ability to tell Spanish pharmacists about her sore throat. Phrases like this can be very useful if you or your baby are unwell abroad.

Handling Common Illnesses and Emergencies

First Aid Kit:

As we discussed above, if you want to, it can be useful to pack a well-stocked first aid kit for babies. Include items like infant paracetamol, a digital thermometer, antiseptic wipes, plasters, and any prescribed medications. I would also advise you to consider packing rehydration sachets in case of dehydration from diarrhoea or vomiting. We have used these sachets a couple times with Evelyn as on one of our trips we travelled from the UK to Spain, and she was getting over a stomach bug she'd had before she left the UK. The sachets really helped, and she was back to normal a day or so after we landed in Spain. I always have a packet of these in our cupboard at home – thank you nursery for the endless illnesses that plague our house.

Managing Minor Illnesses:

As you will know, babies can be prone to minor illnesses like colds, ear infections, or upset stomachs and this can be worrying at any time, but especially when travelling in a foreign country. Knowing how to handle these illnesses can make a big difference. For example, keeping your baby hydrated and rested if they have a cold.

Knowing When to Seek Help:

Trust your instincts. If your baby is unusually irritable, has a high fever, isn't eating or drinking or you're generally worried about their health, don't hesitate to seek medical help. It's always better to err on the side of caution.

When we took Evelyn to Greece, she developed a cough in the car on the way to the airport. I decided it was just a bit of a sore throat and nothing to worry about, so we boarded our flight. Mike had a conference in Cairo, and we were spending a week in Greece before flying to Egypt.

By the time we landed in Athens, Evelyn looked like a sickly Victorian child and her cough was much worse. We went to the pharmacy near our apartment and got her the Greek version of Calpol. During the night, her breathing got worse, and we were monitoring her to see if we needed to take her to hospital. The following morning, she was much improved, and we went to the acropolis and explored Athens. She was under the weather the whole time we were in Greece but seemed to be alright.

When it was time to fly to Cairo, Evelyn slept the whole way, which was unusual as we had a late afternoon flight, and she would normally be awake and alert. By the time we landed in Cairo, she was coughing again, and her breathing seemed erratic. We got to our apartment in Uptown Cairo and Evelyn looked extremely tired. I knew that something wasn't right, and she seemed to be struggling to breathe. We decided to take her to hospital to be looked at.

After taking some advice from a doctor colleague of Mike's who was from Cairo, we got ourselves in an Uber and went to the private hospital that he recommended. As we went inside, they took our driving licence and Mike's credit card at the front desk and told us to collect it from the accounts office on our way out. Thankfully, we had insurance, but we had no idea at this stage what sort of cost we'd be looking at in the interim.

We waited in a small room for about 10 minutes until a nurse came in to examine Evelyn. After they looked her over, they took us straight onto a ward and put Evelyn onto one of the beds and drew the curtains. This was all a bit serious, and we weren't too sure what was happening. I couldn't let anybody know back at home because the phone signal and data situation in Egypt was terrible and everywhere we went seemed to have no public Wi-Fi. It was challenging to say the least.

Around 15 minutes later, a doctor appeared and examined Evelyn again. She then explained that Evelyn had an upper respiratory infection and that they needed to clear her airways. They brought in some equipment and Mike told me to prepare myself because 'they don't do this in the UK'. With that terrifying sentence ringing in my ears, I waited to see what would happen next.

They lay Evelyn down on her side and put a clear tube up her nose and then forced water through it like a hosepipe. Understandably, Evelyn was thrashing around and was very unhappy about the situation she was in. It was quite alarming to watch as it did look to me like she was being waterboarded. Once they'd finished in one nostril, they turned her over and repeated the process. It was quite an ordeal.

When they'd finished, the doctor asked me why I hadn't thought to do this procedure at home… I was too stunned to speak. As soon as Evelyn had stopped shrieking, we were given a prescription for various medications and sent on our way.

We went to the accounts office to pay our bill, and they presented us with an invoice. I am not the best at currency conversion, so we just paid with and left the hospital but when we checked the credit card statement later on, it cost us a grand total of £13. We were in and out of hospital within the hour and the medical team were brilliant. It was alarming to be in that situation in a foreign country where we didn't speak the language, but Evelyn was absolutely fine in the end and it taught me that I could be calm and handle stressful situations like those. Though I hope I do not encounter another one any time soon.

Safety Tips for Different Environments

One of the benefits of travelling is that it introduces your baby to new environments. However, one of the downsides of this is that new environments can pose unique safety challenges. Here's a few tips to keep your little one safe no matter where you are:

Baby-Proofing Accommodation

Check the Room:

When you arrive at your accommodation, it is useful to do a quick sweep and move any hazardous/breakable/shiny items out of reach, secure loose wires, and ensure windows and doors are locked, double check any balcony doors.

Recently Evelyn and I had an absurd experience with an apartment that I could not baby-proof if my life depended on it. I had been asked by a family friend, Sylvia, if I would go to her apartment in Brussels and look after her cats for a week whilst she was out of the country. I agreed as Evelyn hadn't been to Belgium yet and I could work from there remotely.

When we got to the apartment, Sylvia's friend, Sara let us into the apartment. She led us past a door with two suits of armour which were stood menacingly on either side of the door, holding axes. Bemused, I hurried after her and up to the next floor where she opened a door, and we followed her into a corridor.

As we turned the corner, I was stunned. The were tribal masks, intricate paintings, antique vases and even an enormous whale vertebra displayed on a cabinet. Wow. I couldn't believe they had a gallery inside this unassuming building in the centre of Brussels and Sylvia lived so close to it. I followed Sara round the corner ready to leave the gallery and find Sylvia's apartment "Right," said Sara, "this is the living room".

Stunned, I looked at her "Sylvia lives here?!". I couldn't believe it. I had never seen anything like it. There were hundreds of artefacts adorning the walls and every surface. Fragile, expensive, very breakable artefacts. And I had a toddler with me. A wild one. Before I'd had time to process the anxiety that was beginning to creep up inside me, it was time to continue the tour. The apartment was set over two floors and the stairs up to the first floor were huge concrete steps with no banister. If you fell, you were just falling off the side onto the wooden floor 20 feet below. Perfect. Just what I needed with a very mobile toddler who would be sleeping on the first floor with me. With no travel cot to keep her contained.

As I carried Evelyn up the stairs, wondering what on earth I had gotten myself involved in, it got worse. When I reached the rooms on the top floor, I realised that the floor was a U shape, with no doors separating the rooms from the perilous concrete stairs below. I wouldn't even be able to contain Evelyn inside the bedroom at night by closing a door. This was a disaster. How was I going to keep Evelyn alive and unharmed in this place for a week? Everywhere I turned there was another disaster waiting to happen. The dining tables were exactly Evelyn's head height with jagged corners. All of the side tables and coffee tables were glass or made out of golden trumpets.

I went to investigate the other bedroom and found that, not only did it have a series of steep steps leading up to it, as it was on a raised platform, it also had a huge bath built deep into the floor. Evelyn fell into the bath within 10 minutes of us being there and it was a sign of things to come.

After Sara left us, I assessed how best to toddler-proof this expansive apartment. There were so many rooms and so many things that Evelyn could either break or impale herself on. I opted to put cushions on everything that I could, and I blocked the entrance to the top of the stairs with a big chair and some boxes. If she really wanted to, Evelyn could have burrowed her way through the boxes and climbed over the chair, but I was hoping that their presence would be deterrent enough. As I was putting cushions on the floor around the high sofa I heard giggling. I looked up to discover Evelyn sat at the top of the concrete staircase (the one with no banister) waving at me. Brilliant. Another parenting fail.

That was only the beginning of our troubles. We will revisit our trip to Belgium later.

Sleeping Arrangements:

So that you don't end up in a pickle like we did in Brussels, plan ahead. Decide before you go if you're going to be co-sleeping, using a travel cot, or a mixture depending on your accommodation. If you're using a travel cot, make sure it's set up correctly and is free from loose bedding or soft toys. Some hotels offer baby-proofed rooms or cribs, so you can speak to the hotel ahead of time.

If you're using an Airbnb, it is worth double checking with your host that they are providing a cot and checking the cot once you arrive. We recently stayed in an Airbnb in Barcelona and the travel cot was there as advertised, but it was broken and collapsed on one side.

Safety Tips for Various Climates and Terrains

Hot Climates:

Babies are more susceptible to extremes of temperature, so if you're somewhere hot it's important to keep them cool and hydrated. Dress them in light, airy clothing, use sun hats (cute), and apply suncream. Avoid direct sunlight during peak hours wherever possible and stay in the shade as much as you can. If your pram has a sun cover, or a parasol make sure to use it.

If you're using a baby carrier, be mindful of how many layers your baby is wearing as the carrier itself adds another layer of warmth, plus that of the person carrying the baby.

When we were in Lisbon, it was a warm day and Evelyn was in a vest, t-shirt and shorts but she was in her carrier. As we were waiting to board the famous 28 tram in Lisbon, Evelyn proceeded to projectile vomit all over Mike, the other passengers and the street. She had heatstroke.

We took her out of the carrier immediately and stripped all her clothes off. We gave her water and immediately requested an Uber back to our accommodation. We put the air conditioning on full power in the taxi and tried to cool Evelyn down as best we could. She was fine later on that evening, but it was a harsh parenting lesson to us in making sure she is wearing fewer layers if she is in her carrier on a warm day. Or, better still, we can put her in the pram to keep her cool.

Cold Climates:

If you're travelling to colder destinations, it is useful to layer your baby's clothing to keep them warm without them overheating. Ensure they're wearing a hat, mittens, and warm socks or boots. Limit time spent outdoors in extreme cold and be mindful of the risk of hypothermia.

Water Safety:

If you're traveling to a beach or pool destination, always keep a close eye on your baby around water. Use swim nappies and floatation devices if your baby is going into the water, and, of course never leave them unattended, even for a minute.

Urban Environments:

Cities can be busy and overwhelming for your baby (and for you!) if they're not used to them. Use a baby carrier or a sturdy pram to keep your baby safe and comfortable as you travel. Be mindful of traffic and crowded areas, and always make sure your baby is properly fastened in their pram or carrier. Evelyn is prone to unclipping the fastenings on her pram and trying to make a bid for freedom – so keep an eye on them.

Trust your instincts, and most importantly, enjoy the adventures.

Chapter 10

Navigating Airports and Flights

Airport Tips and Tricks

It's the big one - the airport. How do you get through it unscathed?

The airport can feel like an obstacle course at the best of times, let alone when you're travelling with a baby. The information given below should help you navigate airports with ease, you might even have time for a little drink before you take off.

Managing Check-In and Security with a Baby

Arrive Early, but Not Too Early:

I am often known to turn up an hour before departure and it cause extreme stress to everybody that I'm flying with, so give yourself plenty of time to check in. Allow time to go through security and handle any unexpected baby needs. As babies, particularly older babies, have a short patience threshold, so arriving three hours early might be overkill. Aim for a sweet spot of 1.5 to 2 hours. Enough time for a drink and to buy a new book.

Use Online Check-In:

Whenever possible, check in online. It saves time and allows you to choose seats that suit your family's needs. Plus, it's one less queue to tackle with a baby in tow. Some airlines charge a fee if you check-in at the airport and not online so just be aware of that.

With many airlines you are permitted two free items for your baby to check in such as a pram, cot or car seat. These have to be put through the special baggage scanner where they put snowboards and oversized luggage etc.

Family-Friendly Security Lanes:

Many UK airports offer family-friendly security lanes. These lanes are designed to be a bit more understanding of the chaos that comes with travelling with children. Take advantage of them for a less stressful experience and they're often a lot quicker than the queues for the normal security lanes.

Don't waste your money with fast-track passes for the UK airports, you end up in the family lane anyway for free.

Master Security:

Going through security with a baby is like a military operation. Take your baby out of the pram or carrier, fold it up and place all your baby gear on the conveyor belt. Take the milk and baby food out of your bag, take out your own liquids and electricals… go through the scanner… inevitably have your bag searched anyway!

Keeping the baby milk and food near the top of your carry-on bag will help speed up the process. As will using a baby carrier in the

Baby-Friendly Amenities in Airports

Priority Boarding:

 Many airlines offer priority boarding for families with young children. Take advantage of this to get settled in before the rush.

It's a great time to organise your space and make sure you have everything you need for the flight.

Baby Changing Facilities:

Most airports have baby changing facilities in both the men's and women's toilets, as well as in dedicated family rooms. These rooms often have more space and can be a lifesaver when you need to change a nappy or just take a breather.

Once, when Evelyn and I arrived into Vienna Airport, as we are patiently waiting in the queue for border control, Evelyn decides it is the perfect time to have her airport poo. Perfect timing. Of course, it goes everywhere - through her nappy, through her clothes and onto me. A kind lady working at the airport sees this ordeal taking place and waves us to the front of the queue and once we are through we go to the baby changing room. I bin Evelyn's outfit entirely and I get myself fully changed as well.

Once Evelyn's sorted and got her new outfit on, I put her down for a minute thinking I'd seize this opportunity whilst she was contained to have the quickest of wees in the toilet they have inside the changing room. What a mistake. Whilst I was doing this Evelyn decided to wander around exploring the room and had, conveniently, found a big, red cord to pull on. She pulled it before I could react and an alarm immediately sounded and a red light started to flash.

Within seconds there was a man shouting at me in German out of a speaker on the wall. I managed to tell him there was no emergency, just a very mischievous child and we hurried out of there as quick as we could. I noticed as soon as we opened the door that the alarm was not just going off inside the changing room, it was also going off in the corridors complete with flashing lights. People were staring. Brilliant. Mortified, I acted as casual as I could and hurried onto our train into the centre of Vienna. What an entrance into Austria. Wilkommen.

Play Areas:

Some airports do have play areas where little ones can burn off some energy before the flight. Let your baby crawl or toddle around while you relax for a moment, but they will likely need cleaning up afterwards, those floors are filthy!

In-Flight Comfort

Now that you've made it through the airport with your baby and all your bags, it's time to board the plane.

Choosing the Best Seats

Seats at the Front:

If available, the seats at the front of a section with a wall in front can be a great choice. They often have more legroom and can accommodate a bassinet. However, they don't have under-seat storage, so keep that in mind.

Window vs. Aisle:

A window seat can give you a bit more privacy and a place to lean against while feeding your baby. An aisle seat makes it easier to get up and walk the aisles to calm a fussy baby or change a nappy if you need to. Choose based on your baby's needs and your comfort and based on your airline. Some airlines insist that if you are flying with your baby on your lap, you need to be in the window seat.

Top tip: if you're travelling with your partner and you don't want to sit together, book the baby onto their lap and book yourself a seat in a different section of the plane altogether – bliss!

Feeding and Soothing Your Baby During the Flight

Nursing or Bottle-Feeding:

Feeding your baby during take-off and landing can help ease ear pressure. For bottle-feeding, pack enough formula or expressed milk for the journey, plus a bit extra in case of delays. The ready-made formula bottles you can buy in supermarkets or Boots are brilliant for plane journeys.

Snacks and Meals:

For older babies, pack a variety of snacks to keep them entertained and well-fed. Many airlines have meals they offer specifically for older babies or little snack packs which can be great.

Other Items:

Make sure you pack a dummy or a blanket for soothing your baby. Dummies can be good to ease pressure in little ears during take-off and landing.

In-flight Baby Changing

The baby changing in planes is a logistical challenge. It pulls down from the back wall usually and you have very limited arm space to move around whipping nappies off. If you're on a long flight, you can't really avoid using this, but if you're on a short flight, change their nappy just before you board and just after you land and pray there's no reason to change mid-flight!

Dealing with Jet Lag and Time Zone Changes

Adjusting Sleep Schedules:

If you are radically changing time zones and are concerned about your baby's sleep schedules, you can try to shift your baby's sleep schedule a few days before departure to match the time zone of your destination. This small adjustment may help the transition of napping and bedtime schedules.

On-Board Naps:

I am a big fan of encouraging naps during flights, but don't worry too much if they don't go as planned. There's a lot of new things to see and explore and your baby may be too excited to sleep. They can always nap when you land.

Where we can, we try to book flights that are early in the morning or late at night to encourage Evelyn to sleep throughout the flight. This has been an extremely useful tactic when planning our trips.

Stick to Routines:

If your baby has a routine, once you arrive, try to stick to that routine where you can. Keeping loosely to their usual routine can help your baby with the transition to a new time zone.

If your baby is out of sync with their usual routine, don't worry. Travel can be exciting, exhausting and disruptive. Encourage naps where you can at their usual naptimes but accept that these may fall earlier or later than they would at home, and that's okay.

When your baby gets home, they will soon be back into their usual routine, so it isn't the end of the world. Flexibility is your friend when travelling.

Evelyn doesn't really have a routine, which reflects the chaos and lack of structure in my daily life. She doesn't tend to nap during the day when we are travelling anymore because she's desperate to see what's going on around her. This means that we will move her bedtime forward to try and avoid the overtired meltdowns that may follow.

Entertainment and Distraction

Keeping your baby entertained during the flight can be a challenge, but with a bit of creativity, it's entirely possible.

Pack Toys & Books:

Pack a few new toys that your baby hasn't seen before to keep them occupied for longer periods. Small board books can also be a great addition to your hand luggage and don't take up much space. Evelyn has some tiny Little Miss books that she is fanatical about.

Although I don't want to promote excessive screen time, I am guilty of putting Netflix on for Evelyn during longer flights when she's getting irate. A bit of screen time can be a lifesaver on a long flight so you may want to load up your tablet with some programmes or films for your baby.

If I have to watch The Grinch one more time I will scream.

Keeping Yourself Happy

Lastly, don't forget about making sure you are happy on the flight. Dress in comfy clothing, stay hydrated, stay caffeinated and make sure you ask for, and accept, help when it is offered to you by others.

I don't know if it's a British thing of being too polite and willing to struggle alone, but there is often a reluctance to accept help when it's offered. Take it. You need all the help you can get when ferrying a baby and all their gear around with you.

Chapter 11

Accommodation

Choosing the right accommodation can take up a lot of time and you may find that travelling with your baby means that you choose different accommodation than you would if you were travelling on your own.

Hotels, Apartments, and More: What's Best for You and Your Baby?

The good news is you have options. There are plenty of places you can book, from hotels and apartments to B&Bs and family-friendly resorts. Each has its own perks and quirks, so here's a pros and cons list to help you decide what's best for your family.

Hotels

Hotels are the popular choice, and for good reason. They come with a lot of perks including room service, daily cleaning, and a concierge. They often have on-site restaurants, bars, shops, pools, gyms and airport transfers. They can be great.

Pros:

Convenience:

Someone else makes the bed and cleans up, what's not to love when you're on holiday and taking a break from the chores?

Amenities:

Pools, gyms, restaurants, and sometimes even babysitting services if you're feeling brave.

Staff Support:

Need extra towels, a crib, or just a hand with your bags? You can call for someone to help you out.

Cons:

Space:

Unless you get a suite, hotel room are often quite small, especially if you add in a travel cot and all the items you've brought for your baby. If you put your baby to bed in the room, there's not really anywhere for you to go and you may end up having to go to bed at the same time as them. Bed at 7:30pm doesn't sound too terrible to me though...

Cost:

Hotels can be expensive, especially if you need multiple rooms or upgrade to a suite for more space and can be even more depending on your board.

Apartments

For more space and the idea of a home rather than a room, consider renting an apartment. These can be particularly great for longer stays or if you prefer to cook your own meals. I almost exclusively book apartments when I travel now because I have found them extremely useful since having Evelyn for all the reasons given below.

Pros:

Space:

Separate bedrooms, living areas, and sometimes even a garden or a balcony. You can put your baby to bed in their own room and you have other places you can go within the apartment other than straight to bed.

Kitchen:

You have the flexibility to cook your own meals, prep baby food and store snacks (and wine).

Flexibility:

There is much more room to spread out and not feel like you're living on top of each other in one room.

Cons:

Self Sufficient:

Usually, they don't offer daily cleaning or room service, so you're responsible for tidying up and cleaning dishes etc.

Quality:

Unlike hotels, rented apartments can be hit or miss in terms of cleanliness and amenities and once you've booked somewhere you're a bit stuck if you turn up in the middle of the night and don't like the state of the apartment. Whereas in a hotel you can demand a different room.

Availability of Hosts:

A lot of rented apartments give you lock boxes or electronic key codes to allow self-check in. Whilst this does allow you greater flexibility for arrival and departure times, it also means that there isn't necessarily someone to speak to if there's an immediate problem. You often must wait for the host to call or message back which can be frustrating.

Family-Friendly Resorts

If you're looking for a stress-free holiday ticking all the boxes, family-friendly resorts are the perfect option for you. These places are designed with families in mind, offering everything from kids' clubs to baby pools and evening entertainment.

Pros:

All-Inclusive Options:

Meals, activities, and entertainment all in one place.

Child-Friendly Amenities:

Playgrounds, baby pools and evening entertainment.

Other Families:

There are usually lots of other families around, which can be great for encouraging children to make new friends. Or for you to make new friends if you're that way inclined. I am still friends on social media with people we met on holiday in Turkey in 2015. I have never spoken to them since that holiday. I try to keep my head down now when I am lounging by the pool.

Cons:

Cost:

All these perks come at a price. If you're going during peak season or school holidays, it will cost you even more.

Crowds:

Resorts can be busy, especially during peak season and school holidays.

Campervan

That's right. I'm throwing a wild card into the mix for you to consider. A campervan. You can hire them; you can drive your own abroad or you could borrow a friend's. We hired a campervan in Portugal when Evelyn was 8 months old, and we drove it from the top of Portugal to the bottom over a couple of weeks. Despite my initial reservations when we booked it, it was amazing.

We hired our campervan from a company called The Getaway Van in Porto, a small family run business who were fantastic. We didn't have a state-of-the-art campervan, it was essentially a jazzy Ford Transit, but it had everything we needed for adventures on the road.

It had a kitchen, a double bed, another bed in the roof, even an awning and camping chairs to allow you to enjoy a Portuguese sunset of an evening outside your van. We left Evelyn asleep on the double bed inside the van and we would sit outside admiring the views with a couple of glasses of wine.

Our strategy with the campervan was to book campsites as we went, this was to allow us flexibility on the route and to allow us to spend longer in some places if we wanted to. Though, I did book the first night's accommodation, on a vineyard in the Douro Valley, and the final night's accommodation to give us a start and end point.

The places that we stayed during that trip were incredible and inexpensive. I paid £18 for a night in the Douro Valley which also included 2 bottles of wine and a bottle of olive oil. Talk about good value! The most expensive accommodation we paid for was in Lisbon and even then it was less than £60 for the night.

Campervan life is not for everyone, and certainly not for the faint hearted, but it was a brilliant experience and allowed us to see so much more of Portugal than we would have done otherwise. Evelyn had a great time in the van, though she did co-sleep with us the whole time.

We priced up the van vs hiring a car plus the cost of apartments or hotels in each place and the campervan was cheaper and more exciting. We did it for the plot. I would recommend it for those of you who are looking to travel all over.

Top Tips for Booking Baby-Friendly Accommodation

Now that you've got a sense of your options, here are some tips to help you find the perfect spot for you and your little one:

Location

It seems obvious, but when you're searching for accommodation, really do think about where it's located. You'll likely want to be close to the action but because you're travelling with a baby in tow, you probably want to off the noisy main streets whilst also near to some shops in case of food or nappy emergencies.

Proximity to Attractions:

Being near the places you want to visit can save you time and hassle, especially if you aren't there for long. Look for accommodation close to parks, landmarks or the beach. You will pay more for accommodation in these central areas so bear that in mind if you're conscious of budget.

Must-Have Amenities

When booking, make sure to check for baby-friendly amenities that will make your stay more comfortable such as cots, fridges, microwaves, kettles and access to a washing machine (especially if you're on a longer trip).

Read the Reviews

Again, it sounds obvious but I have failed to do this a few times and paid the price for it. Before booking, take a few minutes to read the reviews from other people that have stayed with babies or young children. They'll give you an insight on what to expect and can highlight any potential issues for you ahead of time. If multiple reviews mention noise and hygiene issues, it's an immediate no.

Making the Most of Your Stay

Unpack and Settle In:

When you arrive, it can make your life a lot easier to take some time to unpack and set up your space. Having everything in its place can help you be ready if your baby starts crying for food. You don't want the pressure of a screaming baby when you've not yet unpacked your formula and bottles.

Set Up a Sleep Area:

It is useful to create a sleeping area for your baby when you arrive, whether it's setting up the travel cot or arranging the hotel crib.

Organise Yourself:

Keep nappies, wipes, and other essentials easily accessible. If you're staying in a larger place, designate a baby-changing station. We tend to just change Evelyn anywhere, anytime, but if we were more organised people then we would do that.

Baby-Proof the Space

Even if the accommodation isn't specifically baby-proofed, you can take a few steps to make it safer for your baby by moving hazards and rearranging anything that might be dangerous.

Explore the Area

Once you're settled, the best thing to do is get out and explore! Find nearby parks, supermarkets and coffee shops and get the lay of the land.

Local Insights:

Ask the accommodation staff for recommendations in the area. They can often suggest things that aren't in the guidebooks or online.

Have a Great Time:

You're on holiday – have a glass of wine and chill out!

Chapter 12

Daily Routines and Managing Schedules

Generally, I am not one for set schedules and routines, but I appreciate that these work for people and you may be concerned about how this may look whilst travelling.

Babies can thrive on routines, and while it's impossible to keep things exactly the same as at home, a bit of consistency can help you roughly stick to your schedule. The information below is a guide to help you if you do want to keep a routine on your travels.

Morning Rituals: Starting the Day Right

Mornings set the tone for the day, so let's start as we mean to go on.

Wake-Up Time:

Wherever possible, try to wake up at the same time every day, even when you're travelling. It helps your baby's body clock adjust and keeps things predictable. If you've crossed time zones, ease into the new schedule gradually.

Morning Feed:

Begin the day with a feed. Whether it's breastfeeding, bottle-feeding, or solids, a full tummy makes for a happier baby. If you can, take time to enjoy your morning coffee while they eat. We also want to start the day as **you** mean to go on.

Morning Routine:

Stick to your home routine as much as possible. If you usually have a little playtime, a nappy change, and then get dressed, do the same on the road. These familiar activities help signal to your baby that it's the start of a new day and help them settle in a new environment.

Naps On-the-Go:

Naptime can be one of the trickiest parts of travelling with a baby.

Flexible Nap Times:

While it's ideal to stick to your usual nap schedule, flexibility is key. If your baby usually naps at 10 AM, aim for around the same time, but don't stress if it's a bit later. If you are travelling to another location by plane, car or train try to schedule this around naptime as it may help your baby settle quicker for a nap.

Portable Sleep Solutions:

Following on from the above, a good travel pram or baby carrier can be a lifesaver to encourage babies to sleep on the go. Go for a pram with a good sunshade and a comfy seat or a baby carrier that supports naps. I have the ErgoBaby 360 and it's been brilliant.

Create a Sleepy Environment:

If you head back to your accommodation for nap time, try to recreate the sleeping environment from home. Use blackout curtains, a white noise machine, or a familiar blanket to make your baby feel settled.

Feeding Times:

Feeding your baby on the go doesn't have to be a nightmare and you can handle this with ease if you are prepared.

Breastfeeding on the Go:

If you're breastfeeding, congratulations – you've got the most portable food source. Find a comfortable spot, whether it's a café, park bench, or a quiet corner and away you go.

Bottle Feeding:

For bottle-fed babies, it is slightly trickier. Carry enough formula and sterilised bottles for the day. Most cafés and restaurants are happy to provide hot water to warm bottles. Travel-friendly formula dispensers can make bottle prep easier as well as portable sterilisers or self-sterilising bottles.

The biggest thing we were worried about when we first went away, was how we would deal with making the bottles, cleaning the bottles and sterilising them. If you breastfeed, you've immediately lightened your load significantly on the packing front. Evelyn was bottle fed and I brought the prep machine with me as a non-negotiable item on most of our trips until Evelyn was about 6 months old and needed less bottles during the day. It is the best item I have ever bought.

For those of you who are unfamiliar with the prep machine, it's like a Nespresso machine for babies. Revolutionary. I wouldn't have made it through those first few months without it. My friend Kath loved hers that much that she had two machines in her house, one upstairs and one downstairs.

For sterilising, when we went on our first trip, to France, I brought my giant two-tier MAM sterilising contraption with me. I soon discovered that it does not fit in most European microwaves. It is too tall. So, after all that preparation, we had to sterilise most of the bottles in boiling water on the hob. Like the olden days.

Tip: don't take more than 5 bottles if you are bottle feeding. You really do not need that many, especially if you have the ones that you can sterilise individually in the microwave.

When we went on adventures further afield in the car and were out for the whole day, we took a travel steriliser with us and a portable formula feed set to allow us to sterilise and prepare formula on the go. They make a bottle at perfect temperature within a couple of minutes from boiling water – perfect for when you have an hungry baby who wants feeding **now**. These were one of the best things we bought, and I really do recommend them if you're wanting to travel but also I'd recommend them for going out and about during the day with your babies to the zoo or wherever else. The one I used is by Tommee Tippee but they have a lot of different ones available.

Tip: get a travel steriliser and portable bottle maker.

Solids and Snacks:

For older babies, it is worth packing plenty of snacks and easy-to-eat meals. Some travel-friendly options include rice cakes, fruit pouches, crisps and other easy to handle foods.

Highchair:

A portable highchair can make mealtimes simpler, whether you're in a restaurant or having lunch in the park. I have one by Chicco that cost me about £15 from John Lewis and it is so handy. It folds down small so that you can transport it easily and has two different height settings. It attaches onto normal chairs so it's easy to take with you to restaurants or to other people's homes.

Activity Planning

It may help you to keep to your routine if you plan activities around your baby's schedule. Post-nap, when they're well-rested and fed, is usually a good time for outings. This will depend on the temperament of your baby as well, Evelyn is normally extremely angry when she wakes up from her nap and begrudges being taken to any activities. I can relate.

Evening Wind-Down:

Perhaps the most anxiety inducing part of the day if your baby is not a keen sleeper.

Dinner Time:

Aim to have dinner at a similar time each evening. If you're eating out and your baby is on solids, let them join in the meal. Let them experience new tastes and experiences. If they have their own meal, let them have a little taste of yours, even if it's spicy. They may find their new favourite meal. Evelyn's new favourite food is trofie al pesto, a dish she tried when we returned to Italy most recently. She is, however, quite partial to a curry.

Evening Bath and Bedtime:

It seems obvious but try to stick to your usual bedtime routine as much as possible. Giving your baby bath and a bedtime story like you would at home are familiar activities that signal to your baby that it's time to wind down for bed.

Sleeping Arrangements:

Whether your baby sleeps in a cot, a co-sleeper, or with you, make sure they have a comfortable and safe sleeping environment. If you're staying in multiple places, bring along familiar sleep items like blankets, teddies and sleep sacks.

Extra Patience:

Be patient with yourself and your baby. It might take a few days for everyone to adjust. Stick to your routine as much as possible but accept that some things are out of your control. Try to go with the flow for your own sanity.

Chapter 13

Coping with Stress

Stress. Let's talk about it. Having a baby is an emotional, psychological and physical rollercoaster – there are no two ways about it. They are adorable but they also cause your heart rate to accelerate at least hourly.

Whilst it can be exhilarating to explore new places with your little one, it can be nerve-wracking. You're not alone in this but please know that it does get easier as you do it more. I'd say it gets easier as your baby gets older but, as someone who now has a toddler, I can't say that with any real conviction at this stage.

It's Okay to Be Anxious

It is absolutely normal to feel anxious about travelling with your baby. It is normal to feel anxious leaving the house full-stop with a new baby. You're not alone in this. What if they cry on the plane? What if we run out of formula? What if they get an infection? What if we have forgotten something essential? Take a deep breath. It is fine to feel this way.

Try not to spend too much time on Google and working yourself up further. The internet can be an overwhelming place and may not always help you.

Remember, by taking this trip you are pushing through that barrier of fear and not letting it hold you back from having amazing experiences with your baby. You are feeling the fear and doing it anyway. You should be very proud of yourself, not everybody can do that.

Planning Ahead: Your New Best Friend

One of the best ways to ease anxiety is through planning. While you can't anticipate everything, a bit of preparation can help you feel more in control and more informed about where you're going.

Research:

Research the place you are going, their customs and what to expect. Find out where you can get essentials and where you can access medical care if needed.

Pack Smart:

Make a checklist of baby essentials and double-check it before you leave. I've attached one at the end of this book if you're looking for a rough guide.

Pack extra nappies, wipes, and clothes in your carry-on.

Staying Calm in the Moment: Techniques for Managing Anxiety

Despite all the planning and all the preparation, there will be moments when anxiety creeps in. Here are some techniques to help you stay calm and collected when you feel like screaming into the abyss:

Breathing Exercises:

Simple, yet effective. Hear me out: when you feel anxiety rising, take slow, deep breaths. Inhale for a count of four, hold for four, and exhale for four. Repeat a few times until you feel more centred. I have recently started doing these breathing exercises after facing some stress at work and it has really helped me.

Mindfulness:

If you are somebody who can benefit from mindfulness and quieting your mind, try to stay present in the moment. Focus on the sights, sounds, and smells that are around you. This can help to alleviate anxious thoughts by distracting you and pulling you into the present moment.

My internal monologue is very loud so I find it extremely difficult to practice mindfulness at all, but I know from my Mum, who is very keen on this, that it can be very beneficial to people.

Positive Affirmations:

Remind yourself that you've got this. Repeat positive affirmations like "I am doing my best" or, my personal favourite "I am a boss bitch". I don't know if this works in reality but it makes me feel a lot better either way.

Celebrate:

A victory is a victory no matter how small. You made it onto the plane? Amazing. You got to your accommodation in one piece? Fantastic. Your baby napped when you wanted them to? Incredible. Celebrate your wins.

Use Your Support System:

If you're travelling with a partner, friend, family member or whomever it might be, share the load. Make sure you are taking turns so that you each get some time off to chill, you don't want one person to completely burn out because they haven't been given an opportunity to rest.

I am very guilty of taking on the lion's share of the work and not allowing others to help me. The result is that I feel frazzled and tired. Take help when it is offered and do not be afraid to ask for help when you need it. There are no prizes for martyrdom in parenting – just fatigue.

Self-Care:

Whenever you can, take some time for yourself to rest and recuperate. Do something you enjoy and that you're doing just for you. You might want a nap, some exercise, to binge watch something on Netflix and eat crisps, whatever it is that will put the spring back in your step. I like to belt out Taylor Swift songs in a dramatic fashion, that always makes me feel better.

Stay Hydrated and Eat Properly:

I don't know when I turned into my Mum, but it's happened. I am now nagging you to eat and drink enough. I know it's hard to keep on top of this when you've got a baby demanding your attention all of the time but remember to fill your own cup. Physically and metaphorically.

Get Enough Sleep:

I can't write this with a straight face but stick with me. However, nap when you can and try and go to bed earlier wherever possible. Even an hour of extra sleep can make you feel like a new person.

Embrace the Chaos:

This trip will not go exactly how you imagined it would. Things will pop up and test your patience and resilience. That's part of the adventure and you need to be flexible. Do your best to shake off any difficulties or frustrations that may arise and enjoy the time that you're spending with your baby. I like to consider any 'setbacks' as plot twists, a funny anecdote for a travel book perhaps.

They're only small for such a short period of time and this is time that you will never get back. Enjoy it.

Chapter 14

Cultural Immersion & Language Development

Let's talk about one of the most exciting parts of travelling with your baby – cultural immersion and language development. There's something amazing about seeing the world through your baby's eyes.

Travelling is an incredible opportunity for their growth and development. So, let's chat about how to make the most of your travels to raise a little explorer.

Babies and Cultural Immersion

Babies are like adorable little sponges, soaking up everything around them. This means that travelling offers a unique chance to expose them to different cultures, sights, sounds, and smells, all of which play a crucial role in their development.

Embrace the Local Culture

When you're travelling, try to take the time to immerse yourselves in the local culture. Not only will you create wonderful memories and experience some new things, but you'll also be giving your baby a range of different experiences to learn from as they grow.

Music and Sounds:

The beauty of travelling to different places, is the different types of music you will encounter. This can be street musicians or traditional music in a local café and encouraging your baby to listen to the sounds of the place you're visiting can soothe, entertain, and even teach.

On one of our trips to Spain, Evelyn was absolutely fascinated by some salsa dancers that were performing on the street and did not want to be torn away from them. She was probably their biggest fan in the audience, clapping along very enthusiastically throughout.

Festivals and Events:

If you time your visit during a local festival or event, take your baby along. The colours, costumes, and celebrations will blow their tiny minds. Places like Spain and Italy tend to have multiple festivals and events during the year so have a look if you're hoping to visit one of these countries and see if you can go during a festival.

I have been to the La Tomatina festival in Spain a couple of times, and though I do not recommend it with a baby, it is quite spectacular and one of the most surreal experiences I've had. I stood watching as people tried to climb up a pole covered in grease trying to reach the ham that was on the top. Once someone had made their way to the top, they threw the ham on the ground and signalled the start of La Tomatina.

Trucks then drive through the streets pelting squashed tomatoes at people stood in the streets. Thousands of people are gathered on the streets in this tiny town called Buñol and residents launch tomatoes at people from their balconies and hose them down with water.

People sell giant cups of sangria on the street as well as traditional food from tables that they put up in the middle of the road. It is absolutely chaotic, but it is so much fun. If you ever have the opportunity to go, do. It takes place in the last week of August each year. You can fly into Barcelona or Valencia and take a coach to Buñol.

I would recommend that you let one of the many residents with hose pipes wash the tomato off you before you get the coach back. You will be finding tomato seeds in your hair for days afterwards.

I went off topic with that one, but I had to share it with you.

Back to your baby and their experience:

Local Cuisine:

While your baby might not be ready to dive into spicy curries or exotic dishes, you can still introduce them to new flavours and textures. A bit of mashed banana from a market or some local bread or pastries can be very well received.

Language Development: A Multilingual Journey

As somebody who speaks a couple of foreign languages, I am particularly passionate about this benefit of travel.

Travelling exposes your baby to different languages and sounds which can have a significant impact on their language development. Here's how to make the most of these multilingual opportunities:

Talk, Talk, Talk:

Unsurprisingly, the best way to support your baby's language development is by talking to them. You can constantly describe what you see, hear, what you are doing and where you are going. The more words they're exposed to, the better and it is staggering how much they can pick up in even a short period.

This part comes naturally to me as I am an incessant chatterbox and do talk to myself constantly. I's nice to be able to talk to my baby and simultaneously feel like I am teaching her something useful.

However, Evelyn is unable to say many of the names of our family members but can spot a picture of Taylor Swift from a mile away and will scream 'TAYLOR!'. So I do need to work on what I am teaching her, especially now she's older.

Narrate Your Day:

Talk to your baby about everything. "Look at that colourful flower!" or "Can you see those dogs?" It's all about helping babies make connections and building and expanding their vocabulary as you go.

Reading:

I know we have talked about bringing your baby's favourite books on the trip with you, but you can also think about buying some local children's books. Even if you can't understand every word, the pictures and new sounds can be fascinating for your baby.

Evelyn has a couple of Spanish ABC books and a French one which she loves.

Interact with Locals:

A brilliant way to encourage language development is through interacting with locals. This can be very fun and stimulating for your baby, can give you a bit of a break and equally exposes your baby to new sounds and words in a foreign language.

Plus, it's a great way to make new friends and learn more about the place you're visiting.

If you're quite anti-social and don't like interacting with people full stop, I completely understand that so stick to the other ideas above.

Learn Simple Phrases:

If you're able to do so, try and pick up a few simple phrases in the local language. Greetings, thank you, and please are good starters. Not only is it helpful and polite for you to use these in the country you're exploring, but using these with your baby can help them pick up new sounds and words.

Playtime with Local Kids:

If you meet other families, let your baby play with local children and any children that you may meet. Babies and toddlers love to learn to communicate through play, and it's amazing how much they can learn from each other without speaking the same language.

Incorporate Multilingual Elements at Home:

If you're interested in this aspect for your baby, the language learning doesn't have to stop when you return home. It is easy to incorporate elements of your travels into your daily life to keep the adventure alive by reading the local books you picked up, putting a cartoon on in a foreign language or by taking your baby to some of the language lessons they have available for tots.

There's a class by where I live that teaches babies Spanish from 0-5 years old and I am very keen to enrol Evelyn in these classes.

Similarly, if language learning is a focal point for you as your baby develops, some nurseries have a bilingual or multilingual offering and this can help immerse your child in another language.

There's a nursery local to me that teaches the children in both Spanish and English which will help the children get a grasp on the language at a very young age.

Learning a language can be extremely beneficial in your child's life as they grow older and can open many doors for them.

Songs and Rhymes:

You can sing songs or recite rhymes in different languages. YouTube is a fantastic resource for finding children's songs from around the world. It's another good way to keep up with language exposure if you want to encourage this.

Bilingual Books and Toys:

Invest in some bilingual books and toys. These can introduce your baby to new words and phrases in a playful way.

Evelyn has some toys by Baby Einstein that speak in 3 different languages and encourage babies to learn colours and animals in other languages.

Capturing the Journey

Documenting your travels not only creates lasting memories but can also be a great tool for reinforcing cultural experiences.

Travel Journal:

It goes without saying that I am a big advocate for a travel journal. I like to keep records of where we went, what we did and key moments and lessons from our travels.

That is what allowed me to put this book together.

You can use a travel journal to keep notes and photos of your adventures and, as your baby grows, you can look back at these together and talk about the places you've been and the things you've done together.

Photo Albums:

Create photo albums with captions. Point out people, places, and objects in the pictures and talk about them. This can help reinforce vocabulary and encourage memories as your baby grows.

Another way that you can bring your travels to life is with photobooks. You can easily create these online or through apps on your phone and you can create photobooks to display on coffee tables, bookshelves or wherever you like.

You can look back and reflect on everywhere that you've been. I think that's a great idea because so often the photos that we take on holidays live in our phones or on our social media feeds and they don't make it to our walls.

Stay Curious: Encourage Exploration and Discovery

I have put a large map onto Evelyn's bedroom wall which has most of the countries and various animals displayed on it.

I have printed off polaroids of all of the places that we have been so far and stuck them all around the map to encourage her curiosity about other countries and to allow her to look back at the places we have been as she gets older.

Souvenirs:

I love to buy a little souvenir from everywhere that we visit, whether it's a bauble or a postcard, a bowl or a piece of local art. I like to buy things for the house that I might see or use frequently to remind me of the places that we have been.

At Christmas it's really nice to get all of the baubles out each year and remember trips we have taken and think about the trips we might go on the following year.

I would encourage you to think about these ideas when on your travels and see what works for you.

Chapter 15

Travel Tales

I have lectured you for long enough, it's time to give you some ideas of places that you could visit with your little one and the best way is to give you a flavour of where we have been so far.

From to Andorra to Montenegro, Bosnia and Egypt, to the Netherlands and Slovakia, it has been a hell of a ride.

France: Croissants and Cafés

As you know, France was the first place that we visited with Evelyn when she was a newborn baby.

For accommodation, we rented a 3-bedroom house in the countryside in a tiny town called Saujac in the south of France. Neither of us knew anything about the area when we booked it, but it looked nice enough and it was a great price. We found the house on Airbnb and our host was a lovely Dutch guy called Mees who, conveniently, lived in the house next door.

We pulled up to the house and were amazed by how remote the area was. It was idyllic. Just what we had been hoping for on this first trip. We met Mees who handed over the keys and gave us a tour of the house and he was a lovely man who told us that he had inherited the place after his father passed away during COVID. He lived there with his girlfriend, who baked fresh pastries for us every day, and his mother in law who was from Germany. They had a dog called Max, a very friendly chocolate labrador with a broken leg who would come out to greet us every morning dragging his little cast behind him.

Mees was very eager to know why we would rent his house for a whole month and bring a newborn baby with us. He asked if one of us was writing a book which, at the time, we both found hilarious. I suppose now that my journals have turned into this book, maybe I was writing a book after all and he turned out to be part of our story.

As Saujac was such a small town, we spent a lot of time in the neighbouring town, Cajarc, which had a lot of cafés, restaurants and bars. There was a bridge between these two towns and due to works being carried out on the bridge, you could only drive across it on certain days at certain times. You would risk getting stuck there until the next morning which added a thrilling layer of risk to our trips to the boulangerie and the wine merchant.

Evelyn was particularly popular in the boulangerie, and they would rush over to say "Bonjour Evelyn!" and constantly offer us tiny pastries for her despite her being fresh from the womb and on a milk-only diet.

We used Saujac as our base in France, and we would often go for day trips to visit various towns and places of interest. As Evelyn couldn't stay in the car seat for too long, and because it was very hot, we'd often stop off somewhere obscure on our way to our destination for an emergency bottle or a nappy change.

I dread to think how many nappies I have changed at the side of the road now.

Some of the places we visited during our time in France were incredible. We visited Beaulieu-sur-Dordogne which was a beautiful town in the Dordogne region, and we visited other beautiful towns such as Aubazines, Capdenac, Cabrerets and Saint Criq Lapopie

The weather was fantastic the whole time we were in France and it meant that we were able to walk around and explore so many more places than we would have done otherwise.

One of my favourite places that we visited was Rocamadour. As you approach Rocamadour, the first glimpse of its ancient walls and towering spires takes your breath away. Carved into the rock face, the village appears suspended in mid-air and it is truly spectacular.

Winding cobblestone streets lead you through the heart of Rocamadour, past centuries-old chapels, quaint boutiques, and charming cafés and at the pinnacle of the village stands the revered sanctuary of Notre-Dame de Rocamadour. This is a place of pilgrimage that has been there since the Middle Ages.

We took Evelyn up there in her baby carrier and it's a good job she didn't weigh very much at that time because those steps are very steep. We were exhausted when we made it to the top but the view was absolutely worth it.

Another place that is worthwhile visiting if you get the chance, is Brantôme. It is located in the Dordogne region in southwestern France and it is known as the "Venice of the Périgord" for its picturesque setting along the river.

It is full of beautiful stone bridges which span the river, and ancient buildings line the cobblestone streets covered in ivy and flowers. There are hidden courtyards, incredible restaurants and unique little shops throughout the town.

We also visited the wine region of Cahors and brought back a lot of wine for friends and family, not that we had any room for it!

I had always wanted to visit Mont St. Michel, which is a rocky island located off the coast of Normandy, with an abbey sat on top of the granite cliffs. The abbey is now a major pilgrimage destination in medieval Europe and it dates back to the 8th century.

We visited the small medieval village and walked to the top of the cliffs. Luckily we'd brought Evelyn in her baby carrier because the streets are so narrow and cobbled that our pram wouldn't have made it very far!

Finally, we visited Bayeux to go and see the famous Bayeux tapestry which was something Mike was keen for us to do before we left France. I had my headphones in trying to listen to the audio guide but Evelyn had other ideas so I had to sit outside feeding her whilst Mike made his way to the end of the tapestry. It was quite something.

Our trip to France was amazing and we got to see so many places with Evelyn and it was relatively easy to get around as we were in our car which was definitely the right choice.

Whilst we were in France, we considered if to go further afield and we decided to drive to Andorra.

Andorra: Peaks and Pistes

Neither of us had been to Andorra before but we had heard nothing but good things about it. My aunt and uncle swore that it had the best ski school they'd been to, and they had visited Andorra a lot. Now, I am not gifted, talented or even competent at any sports and cannot ski. But, given we had a 2-month-old baby with us, a stint on the slopes was not on the cards for us. Luckily for me, and for the residents of Andorra.

When we researched further, we saw that Andorra was 4 hours' drive away from where we were staying in France. So, we decided to pack Evelyn back into the car with all her essentials and we drove to Andorra (stopping halfway to give Mike and Evelyn a break from the car).

We stayed there for a few nights, again in an Airbnb that I'd found which was an inexpensive last-minute deal and we stayed in Andorra la Vella which has a lot of alpine scenery and cute cobbled streets. It is the capital city of the tiny principality of Andorra and it was the perfect place for us to take Evelyn as the streets are lined with cafes, boutique shops, and centuries-old buildings colorful shutters.

One of the highlights of Andorra la Vella is the abundance of green spaces, which are perfect for little ones to stretch their legs and burn off some energy. Parc Central is a favourite among families and has playgrounds, picnic areas, and ponds to entertain your baby.

When we went with Evelyn, she was much too young to enjoy anything except looking around at things from the safety of her baby carrier. But I would go back to Andorra again, maybe even to ski next time!

If you drive into Andorra, the scenic drives through the mountains are incredible. We stopped to admire the view at the top of one of the mountains and when we came to start the car again, the battery was flat. It caused a slight panic because we were on the top of the mountain in the middle of nowhere with no signal and a tiny baby.

Eventually, we managed to push the car down the hill and miraculously the engine started again. We thanked our lucky stars because there was nobody else around to help us at that point!

Another test of resilience for us…

Montenegro: Mountains and More

When we got back from our adventures in Andorra and France in November, we felt a sense of accomplishment. We had successfully taken a newborn baby to a foreign country, no, two foreign countries. There were no responsible grownups on hand, and we *survived*. Now, my toxic trait is I like to always have our next trip booked, something to look forward to during the monotony of the 9-5. It irritates Mike enormously. So, high on our first travel victory and with Mike still on parental leave, I decided to up the ante. It was time to go on another trip.

I had a look online for a bit of inspiration and I settled on Montenegro and Croatia. I booked us two weeks travelling around for the following month.

I had never been to Montenegro before and had no idea what to expect. Mike had been before as he'd done a triathlon in Kotor a few years previously and raved about what a beautiful place it is. I did a bit of research and we booked flights from Manchester to Podgorica, the capital of Montenegro. This was going to be our first flight with Evelyn and another parenting test for us.

In Montenegro we hired a car and we spent time in Kotor, Bar, Budva, Sveti Stefan and Hercig Novi. Kotor was my favourite place that we visited because the old town is beautiful and there are lots of great places to explore, especially if the weather is good.

We went in December, so the weather was a bit hit and miss, I'd like to go back in the summer and explore a few more places.

From Montenegro we drove into Bosnia, which was a cool experience, and from there we went onto Croatia.

Croatia: Dalmation Coast & Dubrovnik Dreams

Whilst in Croatia we visited Dubrovnik, Split, Rijeka and then into Zagreb. We'd hired a car and booked Airbnbs in each of those places for ease.

When we were in Croatia, the Fifa World Cup was on and we were in Zagreb in December when the Croatian team came into the city for their homecoming parade. They came in third place and the city was absolutely packed. We saw them on stage and the atmosphere was electric. Evelyn was bundled into her baby carrier watching the fireworks with fascination. It was absolutely freezing as it was mid-December, but it was worth the chills to witness the parade.

Italy: Gelato and Gondolas

When Evelyn was 6 months old, we went to Italy for a week over Easter. We flew into Genoa, where we'd booked an apartment and had a brilliant time exploring the maze of streets in Genoa and eating a lot of pesto.

From Genoa we were able to get the train to Camogli, a beautiful coastal town with restaurants and bars that overlooked the sea. I'd been before the previous year and absolutely loved it so I was keen to take Evelyn and Mike there.

Another place that we visited on the coast called Santa Margherita, go if you get the chance. From there we caught a boat to Portofino. Evelyn was looking like a very bougie baby when we arrived in Portofino, she was wearing her best lemon dress and gingham sunhat and was an instant hit with the locals.

I also took her to Cinque Terre to visit the five coastal towns. We went on a Saturday during Easter weekend and although it was amazing to see all of the towns and the colourful houses in the cliffs, it was packed. I would definitely recommend going out of season for that one. September was a good time of year to go, the crowds were a lot smaller when I went the previous year.

Evelyn took to Italian life like a duck to water. She was starting to eat solids at this stage, so she was thrilled to sample her first piece of focaccia and her first pistachio ice cream.

We have taken Evelyn to Venice, Rome, Florence, Lake Garda and many places in between. Italy is one of the most baby-friendly countries we've been to and that's why we keep going back.

Spain: Siestas and Sunshine

We have been to a couple of places in Spain so far. Starting in Calpe on the Costa Blanca, we went out for a week to stay in a villa with family for my Mum's 50th birthday. My brother and his fiancée Amy came along as did my Grandma and Stepdad, Rob.

Staying in a villa was perfect for us with Evelyn and the place we stayed had floatation devices for babies, arm bands, life jackets and the works. She absolutely loved floating around in the pool in her inflatable penguin being terrorised by Uncle Jacob.

Going away with family was a revelation. So many people to lend a hand with Evelyn and offers to babysit so that we could go out for the night baby-free.

I recommend going away with family at some point if you can do so as you're much more likely to get chance to relax than if you just go it alone with your baby!

We recently went to Barcelona where I ran the Barcelona Marathon. I love that city as it is teeming with vibrant culture and stunning architecture. It is a very baby friendly city and the food is incredible.

Evelyn was fascinated by the Sagrada Familia, which you could see from the window of our apartment, and she loved cheering me on during the marathon. She even tried to run alongside me at one point when I came past her, it was a lovely experience, even if I was on Struggle Street towards the end.

Tip: Spain's love for siestas can work in your favour. We found that the quiet afternoons were perfect for our baby's naps, allowing us to nap or enjoy a sangria on the terrace.

Portugal: Port and Pastel de Nata

After the success of our trip to Italy, I got overconfident. I decided that we had this baby travel thing under control. There was nothing we couldn't do.

This brings us onto the trip that made me question both my parenting skills and my sanity. Portugal. The backstory to this trip is that our friends Sam and Jane had a baby a few weeks after Evelyn was born, and they had also chosen to spend their parental leave abroad. They were spending 4 months in Portugal. Once I heard about this excellent use of time off work, I was very keen to go over to Portugal to visit them and to meet baby Hugh. I had never been to Portugal before, but I had always wanted to go, and this seemed like the perfect time.

Sam, Jane and baby Hugh were staying in Sagres, on the Algarve, and we decided that we would fly into Porto and travel all around Portugal before making our way down to the Algarve to visit them.

We went to Portugal in May 2023 and, as you know, we lost the plot and hired a campervan. After we collected our campervan in Porto, we headed to, Braga. This was a few miles north of Porto and it had been recommended to us as a place to visit. The journey to Braga took us up some very tight, winding roads that led us up many hills. It wasn't the best introduction to van life as our heavy van did struggle to make it to the top. There were a few hairy moments on our way up. And a few more when we tried to park it.

We then made our way into Douro Valley where we spent a couple of days exploring the vineyards and enjoying the Portuguese sunshine before heading down to Aveiro which is nicknamed the Venice of Portugal.

When we arrived in Aveiro I was blown away by all the little bridges over the canal which were covered in hundreds of brightly coloured ribbons. The idea was to write your names on the ribbons and tie them to the bridge, an alternative to the love lock bridges. I immediately bought a ribbon from one of the little shops we saw and set about writing our names on it and tying it to the bridge. If you ever get a chance to go to Aveiro, make sure you do. It's got fantastic bars, restaurants and shops and it's very pram-friendly.

After our trip to Aveiro we drove down to Sagres to meet Sam, Jane and baby Hugh. The drive wasn't terrible down to the Algarve, as Portugal isn't a huge country. I think you can drive the whole of it top to bottom in about 6 hours. The tolls were expensive for getting down to the Algarve, so bear that in mind if you're considering driving in Portugal.

When we got to Sagres we spent the day with Sam, Jane and Hugh. It was really sweet watching Evelyn and Hugh interacting with each other. Sam and Mike were wearing matching baby carriers whilst Jane and I had a few well-earned drinks. It was great to catch up with them as they lived in Dublin and we hadn't seen them for months, since Jane and I were both pregnant at our friend's wedding the previous year.

After our time in Sagres, and after Evelyn had spent hours playing on the beach, we started our journey back up towards Porto where we would eventually be dropping our campervan off.

We stopped off at Porto Covo to visit the beach and Evelyn absolutely loved it. It was a hidden gem on the route. From Porto Covo we went to Evora which has a church made of bones on the inside. It was quite something and very unsettling.

During our research of Portugal, Mike mentioned that he wanted to visit Nazaré, a town known for its huge waves which attract hundreds of surfers to the area. We were able to stop there overnight to see the waves.

The best place that we went during our trip to Portugal was Lisbon. The Time Out Market was phenomenal, and we all ate so much food. There's a lot to see and do so it's an ideal place to stay for a long weekend.

After Lisbon we went to Porto to return our campervan and stayed there until our flight home. Porto was brilliant, we went port tasting (of course) and wandered the narrow streets eating all the Portuguese food we could get our hands on.

We'd been told to try a francesinha in Porto (a fancy meat toastie) and we were very excited to try it. I had two. They were delicious, and I absolutely recommend them if you visit Porto.

Egypt: Pyramids and Pharaohs

Recently, Mike had been invited to a work conference in Cairo and Evelyn and I decided to tag along as none of us had been to Egypt before and it seemed like a good opportunity to visit.

The conference was in November so we thought the weather would be ideal for Evelyn at that time of year. After our dramatic trip to hospital on the first night, the rest of the trip was great.

We booked a trip to the pyramids of Giza through Viator, and we were collected by a private vehicle and we had a private tour guide. She took us to the pyramids, and we went inside the second pyramid which was fascinating and also a tight squeeze for Mike who is over 6ft tall and had Evelyn strapped to the front of him. The entrance is steep and narrow and we did struggle slightly to get in and out.

Our guide was fantastic – she was really friendly and knowledgeable and even had Evelyn on her knee during the car journey, pointing the camels out to her.

I took Evelyn on the camel ride with me, in her baby carrier. It took quite some doing to try and climb onto the camel with one hand on the saddle and one hand trying to stop Evelyn tipping out the side of the carrier. Eventually we managed it and we were off. The expressions on the faces of people coming towards us were priceless when they saw Evelyn strapped to the front of me on this huge camel.

After the camel ride we visited the Sphynx and Evelyn was getting a bit hot and overtired at this stage so we cut the tour short before the planned stop at the papyrus factory and took her back to our apartment.

Despite the bumpy start to our Egyptian adventure, we had a fantastic time and will treasure those memories forever.

Tip: Consider visiting major sites early in the morning or late in the afternoon to avoid the peak heat and crowds.

Belgium: Frites and Fairytales

Here we are once again, we've returned to Belgium and most unsafe apartment I've ever stayed in.

As you know, Sylvia's friend Sara had been showing us where everything was in her apartment, and I had been asked to feed her cats. Now, I have a cat. A very cute little tortoiseshell called Simba. I like cats, I can look after cats.

Sara went on to show us where the cat food was and gave me instructions about when they were to be fed and their temperaments. That was all fine, very straightforward. Then, things took a turn. "Here's the Onslow Protocol" Sara said, handing me a laminated piece of paper with a list of instructions on. The Onslow Protocol? It sounded like something from a James Bond movie.

As I read the piece of paper, my slight feeling of generalised anxiety from this dangerous apartment increased tenfold. It turned out that Sylvia's cat had leukaemia and I was required to administer chemotherapy to him three times a week as well a series of other medications twice a day. Nobody had mentioned this to me when I had agreed to mind the cats. I thought it would be a situation where I put food and water out a couple of times a day and that would be that.

Luckily, so far, I have never had to administer any medication to Simba in her 3 years on this earth. Unluckily, it meant that I was woefully unprepared to cosplay as a vet for this cat with a serious medical condition. The stakes seemed quite high and poor Onslow had been left in my incapable hands.

"HIYA!" Evelyn broke my trail of thought as she chased poor Onslow out of the kitchen, and he fled up the concrete staircase. If he didn't die from my veterinary skills, or lack thereof, he would almost certainly die of fright.

We spent the afternoon wandering around Brussels, seeing some sights, eating a lot of food and visiting some of the amazing shops they had. I ended up with armfuls of knick knacks and pieces of jewellery from lovely independent shops. It was a shame I'd just brought a backpack with me because I really had no room for them.

When we got back to the apartment, it was time for Onslow's first dose of medication. I studied the instructions on the Onslow Protocol and got the tablets out. How was I going to get this cat to cooperate with me? He'd never seen me in his life, and I was about to pick him up and try to wrestle medication into his mouth. What could go wrong? I enticed him over by putting some food out and managed to pick him up, he was quite heavy for a cat. I sat him on the table and managed to open his mouth with one hand and tried to get the tablet to the back of his throat with my other hand. It took 5 attempts and a lot of meowing and wriggling from Onslow whilst Evelyn stood next to us, clapping enthusiastically and shouting "MEOW!". Great, one dose down. Only a dozen to go this week.

Miraculously, we survived our first night in the tower of terror with no injuries. The next day we gave Onslow his medication, with slightly more success than the previous day's dose, and we went off to explore Brussels. Evelyn was thrilled to have a Belgian waffle smothered in Biscoff, I was less thrilled to clean it off every surface and both of us.

We returned to Brussels that evening and it was time to face the music. According to the Onslow Protocol it was time for me to administer the first chemotherapy treatment. After some hunting around the apartment, I discovered Onslow hiding under a chaise longue in one of the bedrooms. Understandable, given Evelyn's eagerness to cuddle him. The Protocol gave me very specific instructions: the chemotherapy medication is kept in the fridge. Wash your hands twice before putting your latex gloves on. Administer the medication and absolutely do not under any circumstances let it touch your skin. Wash your hands after disposing of gloves. Fine. I can do this. What could go wrong?

I washed my hands, put my blue latex gloves on and got the medication out of the fridge and into my syringe. I managed to pick Onslow up and put him on the table, trying to secure him with one arm and wielding my syringe in the other. Neither of us was very happy about the situation we found ourselves in. Onslow started to wriggle around trying to jump off the table as I was bringing the syringe closer and I was trying to keep hold of him and give him the medicine. In all of the struggle he managed to jump out of my grasp and knocked my arm with his hind legs as he scarpered, knocking the syringe of chemotherapy straight into my face. Perfect.

I immediately washed and scrubbed my whole face to try and remove any chemo residue and tried to administer Onslow's medicine again. This time we were successful, and he sauntered off to have his evening meal. I decided to Google what will happen if cat chemotherapy treatment gets onto your skin and accepted from the internet strangers that I was doomed.

The next few days passed in Brussels passed without any major incidents and I thought maybe we were out of the woods. Onslow had not shuffled off this mortal coil yet and neither had I. Things were looking up. Until I started brushing my hair one morning and a large chunk of it came out into my brush. I thought 'this is it, it's happening'. Thankfully, it turned out that my hair was just in terrible condition. Panic over. Note to self: book a hair appointment ASAP.

The Netherlands: Tulips and Canals

Following the stress of our few days in Brussels, I decided that it would be a great idea to get the Eurostar from Brussels to Amsterdam. Evelyn hadn't yet been to Amsterdam and I had only been once before. The train journey was under two hours and we got an early morning train that got us into Amsterdam at around 9am. I took the travel pram and a small backpack with us that just had a few nappies, a couple of outfits, some wipes and a dummy.

The train journey was very smooth, Evelyn had a banana and some pastries on the train just after we left Brussels and after a bit of grumbling she slept for most of the journey as we'd set off quite early and she was not keen to be woken up at that time. The irony. We got out of the station very quickly and found ourselves in the centre of Amsterdam. Evelyn was ravenous once again so we stopped at a pancake house so that she could cover us both in chocolate sauce and refuse to eat her expensive pancakes.

We power walked around Amsterdam after our pancakes, keen to see as many of the sights of the city as we could. It's a very pram friendly city and every bar and café that we went in, people went out of their way to look after us and interacted with Evelyn. It was a really great place to take a baby to and the majority of places had good baby changing facilities.

When I first came to Amsterdam, with a couple of my friends, we went one of the boat trips because the weather was lovely. I would recommend doing that if you ever visit because it's a great way to see all the different parts of Amsterdam and they usually have a guide talking you through all of the different areas and the points of interest. This can be very useful if you don't have loads of time there. I decided to walk along the canals this time and we visited some beautiful parks so that Evelyn was able to run around and let off some steam. It's a beautiful city and the canals are quite spectacular.

When I visited Amsterdam with my friends, we decided in a moment of madness that we should all get matching tattoos. We were caught up in the excitement and at the time the cliché felt like the Best Idea Ever. After some research online, we found a place that did small tattoo designs in a gumball machine. The idea was that you had a coin, you span the wheel and whatever tattoo came out the other side, that was what you were having. This was even better than matching tattoos we thought.

We'd seen inside the shop what designs were on offer in the gumball machine and some of them made us a little nervous. There was one design I was very keen to get, a cat wearing a ruffled collar round its neck. I was also quite drawn to the goldfish in a bag design. We paid our money inside the shop and collected our coins. The tattoo I ended up with is not great, but it could have been so much worse.

This trip I decided not to pay a visit to the gumball machine as I was in sensible mum mode, but we did take a wrong turn which ended up in an impromptu visit to the red light district. Evelyn was sat in her pram waving at the ladies in the window and they mostly waved back. It was a moment of questionable parenting and we quickly walked back into the main square.

There is an attraction in Amsterdam called the Upside Down and it's an immersive experience that has upside down designs and optical illusions. It has ball pits, swings, a pink plane, costumes for dressing up and much more. It's a good rainy-day activity and a fun place for children. You can scan your code on your phone as you enter each room in the experience and you will have access to all of the photos taken at the end for free. For adults, on Fridays and Saturdays they have cocktail combo tickets and a live DJ. It's well worth a visit if you get the chance.

If you're a thrill-seeker, another attraction that is worth doing is going to the Ad'm Lookout swing where you are hoisted high above the buildings on a large mechanical swing that swings you out over the top of Amsterdam and you can see the city all around you. If you're afraid of heights, this probably isn't one for you.

Our trip to Amsterdam was just the tonic to settle our nerves after the rollercoaster that had been Brussels, and it was another country that Evelyn had ticked off her list.

Chapter 16

Budgeting & Financial Tips

Let's talk money. Travelling with a baby can seem expensive when you factor in all the equipment, flights and accommodation. However, if you're organised and smart about it, it doesn't have to break the bank. I have given some tips below to help make travelling more affordable.

Instead of going on one luxurious holiday a year, I tend to book cheaper trips and go on more of them throughout the year. This is partly because the idea of staying in one place or a resort for a couple of weeks doesn't usually appeal to me and also because I prefer to travel around to a few different places.

I appreciate that everybody is different and, to some people, the idea of driving a campervan round Portugal is their idea of hell!

Planning Ahead:

For flights and accommodation, you want to book these early, but not too early. Much like arriving at the airport, there's a sweet spot.

Flights:

Many airlines have deals and flash sales so make sure you're signed up for their marketing emails. I also use Jacks Flight Club which is great for deals on longer haul flights.

Ideally you want to book your flights 3-6 months before you go or, a week or two before if you're a last-minute person like me. I often get very cheap flights if I am going last minute and can be flexible on dates (i.e. not the weekend flights).

For babies, most airlines will charge a fee for your baby to sit on your lap and it tends to be around £25 per flight so keep this in mind when factoring in your costs.

If flights to your destination are expensive, it's worth looking at nearby airports and seeing if you can get there quickly and inexpensively by train. Italy is a good example of this as their transport network is brilliant and you can get from one side of the country to another very quickly.

Accommodation:

For accommodation, consider booking well ahead, especially if you're travelling during peak season. Websites like Booking.com and Airbnb often have early-bird discounts.

Travel Off-Peak

If you can be flexible with your dates, travelling off-peak can save you a lot of money. Avoid weekend flights, school holidays and peak season if possible to get the best prices.

Why Off-Peak?

Not only are flights and accommodation cheaper, but attractions and restaurants are also less crowded, making for a more relaxing experience.

Use Points and Miles

If you've got loyalty points or air miles, now's the time to use them. Sign up for airline and hotel loyalty programmes – they can offer significant savings.

Accommodation

Choosing the right accommodation is key to keeping costs down and ensuring a stress-free stay for you and your baby.

Consider Self-Catering

Staying in self-catering apartments or houses can be a game-changer.

Why Self-Catering?

You can prepare your own meals, which is not only cheaper but also more convenient with a baby. Plus, you'll have more space for all baby essentials.

Family-Friendly Hotels

Some hotels go the extra mile for families. Look for places that offer free cots and highchairs.

Tip: Many family-friendly hotels offer packages that include meals and activities, which can save you money in the long run.

Eating Out

Food is often a big part of the travel experience, but dining out all the time can add up. Here's how to enjoy local cuisine without overspending.

Mix It Up:

Balance eating out with self-catered meals.

Markets and Supermarkets:

Visit local markets and supermarkets to stock up on essentials. Preparing simple meals can be easy, convenient, and save you money.

Lunch Over Dinner:

If you want to try that fancy restaurant, go for lunch instead of dinner. Many places offer cheaper lunch menus with the same delicious food.

Street Food and Picnics:

Embrace the local street food. It's often cheaper and just as tasty as sit-down meals. Take advantage of parks and scenic spots for picnics. It's a great way to enjoy the local scenery and give your baby some time exploring outdoors while keeping costs down.

Getting Around: Transport Tips

Transport costs can add up quickly, but there are ways to travel smart.

Public Transport:

Public transport is usually the cheapest way to get around.

Why Public Transport?

Buses, trams, and trains are often more affordable than taxis, and many cities offer family passes or discounts. Use apps like CityMapper and Rome2Rio to find out how to get from A to B. Use apps like Omio to book train tickets easily which are then saved onto your phone for ease. Use local taxis as well as apps such as Uber and Bolt in major cities.

Walk Whenever Possible:

Walking is a fantastic way to explore new places. Plus, it's great for getting your baby to nap on the go and for getting your steps in. I maintain that it's the best way to see a city.

Car Hire: To Rent or Not to Rent

Sometimes hiring a car can be cost-effective, especially if you're planning to explore rural areas or multiple destinations. We often hire a car on our travels as it has been a lot easier to transport luggage from place to place, it allows us to stop at unusual places and it gives us more freedom and flexibility to change plans as we go. You can also see if your hire car company lets you hire a baby car seat to save you bringing your own on the plane.

Tip: Look for deals and book in advance. Also, check if your accommodation offers free parking.

Baby Gear: Travel Light

Travelling with a baby means extra gear, but you don't need to bring everything with you. Pack only the essentials to avoid extra baggage fees.

Multi-Use Items:

Look for multi-use items like a travel cot that doubles as a playpen or a pram that converts into a bassinet.

Rent or Borrow Items:

Consider renting or borrowing baby gear at your destination.

Why Rent?

Websites like BabyQuip offer rentals for everything from prams to highchairs, saving you from lugging everything with you.

Free Activities: Fun Without the Price Tag

You don't have to spend a lot to have a good time. Many destinations offer free or low-cost activities that are perfect for families

Parks and Playgrounds:

Take advantage of local parks and playgrounds. They're great for letting your baby burn off some energy while you relax.

Museums and Cultural Sites:

Many museums and cultural sites offer free entry on certain days or have discounts for families.

Tip: Check online for free days or special family rates before you go. Also consider apps like Viator or Get Your Guide to book excursions and activities in advance at discounted prices.

<u>Local Events and Festivals:</u>

Look out for local events and festivals. They often have free entertainment and are a great way to immerse yourself in local culture if you're so inclined.

Chapter 17

Tech, Tools & Resources

Let's talk tech and explore some must-have tools for your travels.

Apps:

Let's start with apps that can save you loads of time and stress. Here are some that are perfect for travelling with a baby.

Baby Tracker Apps:

Not as unsettling as they sound, these apps allow you to keep track of feeds, naps, and nappy changes while on the go. Baby tracker apps like Baby Connect or Huckleberry are good options if you are somebody who likes to track throughout the day.

Why Use Them?

These apps let you log all information about your baby, so you can keep an eye on your baby's schedule and how much they're eating even when you're in a different time zone. I am really bad at putting information into these apps so I have never really used them, but I know some parents swear by them!

Navigation Apps:

Getting lost with a baby in tow is not fun. Make sure you've got reliable navigation apps like Google Maps or similar on your phone.

Tip: Google Maps is great for finding baby-friendly spots like changing facilities, parks, and family-friendly restaurants. Just type in what you're looking for, and off you go.

Language Translation Apps:

If you're travelling to a country where you don't speak the language, apps like Google Translate can be incredibly handy.

Why Use Them?

You can translate text, speech, and even signs. Plus, the app works offline if you download the language pack beforehand – perfect for when you're in areas with dodgy service or no Wi-Fi.

Baby-Friendly Travel Apps:

There are apps designed specifically to help parents find baby-friendly facilities and activities. Try Baby Travel UK or BabyOut for tips on the best places to go with your little one.

What Do They Offer?

These apps provide reviews and recommendations for family-friendly attractions, restaurants, and accommodation. It's like having a local guide who understands the needs of parents.

Entertainment:

Keeping your baby entertained while travelling can be a challenge, but there are plenty apps that can help you out.

White Noise Apps:

If your baby struggles to sleep in new places, a white noise app can be a game-changer. Apps like White Noise Baby or Sleepy Sounds can help create a soothing environment. There are also a lot of soothing playlists and lullaby playlists available on Spotify. My favourite is Sparrow Sleeps which offers lullaby versions of modern songs and even some retro songs you haven't heard in years.

Tip: These apps offer a variety of sounds. Find out what works best for your baby and keep it handy for naptime and bedtime.

Educational Apps:

Every day is a school day here…

For older babies and toddlers, educational apps like Peekaboo Barn or Fisher-Price's Laugh & Learn series can entertain your baby.

Why Use Them?

They're great for keeping little ones occupied during flights or long car rides, and they offer interactive learning through play.

Portable Entertainment Devices

As we know, a tablet or smartphone can be a lifesaver, especially on long journeys. Load it up with apps, videos, and e-books before you go.

Tip: Invest in a good, durable case and screen protector. Evelyn is like Godzilla and has demolished one laptop, one iPad and one phone so far. I did not have cases for my gadgets and learnt my lesson the hard way.

Tech Gadgets: Must-Have Travel Gear

Now let's talk about some gadgets that can make your life easier when travelling with a baby.

Portable Bottle Warmers:

Finding a way to warm bottles on the go can be tricky. Portable bottle warmers, like the Tommee Tippee Travel Bottle and Food Warmer, or Formula Feed Maker are so convenient. I honestly would not have survived our travels without them and cannot recommend it enough.

How They Work:

These gadgets use hot water to warm up bottles or food jars, making them perfect for day trips or flights. The formula feed maker turns hot water into perfect temperature within a couple of minutes allowing you to make formula quickly on the go. It comes with a pot that allows you to premeasure your formula on the go.

Travel Baby Monitors:

A compact, portable baby monitor can give you peace of mind when staying in hotels or with friends and family. Look for ones with good battery life and a decent range.

Why Use Them?

They allow you to keep an eye (or ear) on your baby while you relax in another room.

Itinerary Management:

If you're a Type A personality and want to keep track of flights, hotel reservations, and activities, apps like TripIt or Google Trips can help you organise all your travel details in one place.

Tip: Forward your confirmation emails to these apps, and they'll create a detailed itinerary for you, complete with maps and directions.

Health Apps:

Apps like NHS Direct or WebMD Baby can provide valuable health information and advice.

Why Use Them?

They offer a lot of information on baby health, from common illnesses to developmental milestones, and can help you decide when to seek medical attention.

Chapter 18

Different Types of Travel: City Sights vs. Rural Delights

Let's get into the nitty-gritty of different types of travel: city escapes versus rural retreats. Both have their own unique charms and challenges, especially when you're travelling with a baby. Whether you're navigating bustling city streets or soaking in the serenity of the countryside, or basking on a lounger at an all-inclusive resort, there's plenty to enjoy and a few things to keep in mind.

City Escapes: The Urban Jungle

Cities are vibrant, dynamic, and packed with things to see and do. From iconic landmarks to famous museums, vibrant markets to fancy restaurants, there's never a dull moment. But how do you manage the hustle and bustle with a baby in tow?

Pros of City Travel

1. Convenience at Your Fingertips:

Everything you need is usually just around the corner. Pharmacies, baby supply shops, and medical facilities are easily accessible.

2. Public Transport:

Cities generally have excellent public transport systems. Trains, buses, and trams make it easy to get around without needing to bring a car seat.

3. Endless Activities:

This is a big one and very much depends on your personality and your preference when travelling. There's no shortage of things to do. This can either be exciting or overwhelming depending what camp you're in. In terms of things to do for your little one, there are parks and playgrounds and child-friendly museums and zoos. You'll have plenty of options to keep your little one entertained whatever the weather.

4. Accommodation Choices:

You'll find a wide range of accommodation options, from budget-friendly hotels to luxury apartments. Many hotels in cities cater specifically to families with young children and provide travel cots and other baby essentials.

Cons of City Travel:

1. Crowds and Noise:

Cities can be noisy and crowded, which might be overwhelming for your baby (and you!).

2. Limited Green Spaces:

Finding quiet, open spaces for your baby to play might be more challenging. When we went to Barcelona recently, we struggled to find green spaces or parks for Evelyn to play in.

3. Cost:

Cities can be expensive. From dining out, travel and attractions, the costs can add up quickly.

Tips for City Travel

1. Plan Ahead:

A common theme in this book. Make sure to research baby-friendly attractions and facilities before you go. Many museums and galleries offer special activities for young children.

2. Use a Baby Carrier:

A baby carrier can be more practical than a pram in busy areas, especially if you're using public transport.

3. Stay Central:

Choose accommodation that's centrally located to minimise travel time to the main attractions.

Rural Retreats

Rural destinations offer peace, a place of calm away from the chaos of city living and a chance to spend time in nature. But is it the right place for you and your baby? Let's find out.

Pros of Rural Travel:

1. Peace and Quiet:

The countryside is a breath of fresh air, and the slower pace and quieter environment can be calming for both you and your baby.

2. Open Spaces:

This gives plenty of room for your baby to crawl, toddle, and explore. Plus, the natural surroundings can be a great sensory experience.

3. Fresh Air and Nature:

Rural areas offer beautiful landscapes and fresh air. Perfect for outdoor activities like picnics, hikes and other outdoor activities. This can be a big selling point if you don't live in an area where this is easily accessible and want a chance to spend some time outdoors.

4. Lower Costs:

Generally, rural destinations are more affordable. You can find lovely accommodations and enjoy activities that don't cost anything. We recently rented a house in the middle of nowhere in Italy and it cost less for a week there than it did for a night in Venice.

Cons of Rural Travel:

1. Limited Facilities:

There will be fewer shops, restaurants, and medical facilities. If you do opt for a rural destination, it is important to try and pack everything you might need.

2. Transport Challenges:

Public transport options might be limited, so you'll probably need a car. This means increase in costs and the added complication of dealing with car seats and navigating winding country roads.

<u>3. Less Variety:</u>

While the countryside is beautiful and has its charm, there might be fewer attractions and activities, especially if you're used to the hustle and bustle of city life. I love the variety that staying in a city affords you and I do struggle to stay in rural areas for too long. Conversely, Mike hates cities and would always stay in rural areas if he could. We have to compromise a lot when choosing travel destinations.

Tips for Rural Travel

<u>1. Pack Smart:</u>

Bring all the essentials, including nappies, baby food, and any specific items your baby needs. Don't rely on local shops to have everything.

<u>2. Car Essentials:</u>

Make sure your car is equipped with a good car seat and consider renting a car with SatNav if you're unfamiliar with the area or Bluetooth so that you can connect your own navigation system from your phone.

<u>3. Explore Nature:</u>

Take advantage of your surroundings. Go for walks, explore local farms, and enjoy outdoor playtime with your baby. Let them experience this new environment!

Balancing Both: The Best of Both Worlds

Why choose just one? Combining city and rural destinations in your travel plans can offer a balanced and enriching experience for you and your baby. As I said above, Mike and

I like very different things when travelling to a new destination. Here's how to make the most of both:

City First, Countryside Later:

Start your trip with a few days in a city to enjoy the sights and activities, then head to the countryside for some relaxation and nature.

We recently went to Venice for a few days and then went to Lake Garda and then into Florence for a few days and then into Umbria in the countryside before heading to Rome. It was a really good mix of city hustle and bustle and calmer days in the countryside to recover and take a breath.

Day Trips:

If you're staying in a city, consider taking day trips to nearby rural areas. This way, you get a taste of both without having to switch accommodation.

Stay Flexible:

Be open to changing your plans based on how your baby is coping. If the city feels too overwhelming, a quick escape to the countryside might be just what you need to recover.

Chapter 19

Seasonal Travel

Travelling and navigating the changing seasons – each season offers new adventures for you and your baby. From frosty winters to scorching summers, your baby will enjoy experiencing it all.

Spring:

When the sun begins to peek out from behind the clouds, flowers are finally blooming, and it's Aperol Spritz time once again. Spring is one of my favourite times to travel, especially around Europe.

What to Expect:

Flowers:

From the tulip fields in Holland to cherry blossoms in Paris, spring is a beautiful time of year and brings a lot of colours for your baby to experience.

Weather:

In spring the weather starts to improve, and you no longer have to leave the house in 5 layers. Travel during the spring months will likely mean it is the perfect temperature for your baby. Not too hot and not too cold. Spring is the Goldilocks of the seasons. Drier weather means babies can make use of parks and playgrounds and spend a lot more time outside. This can make it much easier to entertain your little one.

Once, we took Evelyn to Genoa over Easter and it was absolutely pouring down for two days and we had to take her to the aquarium for hours just to keep her entertained. We timed it horribly.

Baby Animals:

Another great thing about spring is the flurry of baby animals. Your baby can meet piglets, ducklings, lambs and more. Evelyn currently has a fascination with horses and will stand happily at a gate shouting 'horsie!' until you drag her away or the horse runs from her.

Tips for Spring Travel:

Layers:

Weather can be unpredictable in spring, especially if you're travelling in Europe, so dress your baby in layers to adapt to changing temperatures. Consider that it will be much cooler in the evenings than at midday.

Prepare for Rain:

If you're reading this and you're from the UK, this is written into your DNA anyway. Bring a raincoat for your baby and a rain cover for your pram or baby carrier.

Summer:

Before I had Evelyn, this was my favourite season. Now it is a nightmare because of how sensitive babies are to the sun and hot temperatures. I exist in the shade only.

Longer days mean lighter nights and can mean more difficulty getting babies to sleep. Blackout curtains are your best friend.

That being said, it is great for babies to be outdoors, in swimming pools and paddling pools and enjoying putting their little toes on the sand.

What to Expect:

Sunshine:

It's the time for outdoor activities, swimming, going to the beach, paddleboarding, and eating every meal outside. It's finally BBQ season.

Longer Days:

You can go on evening walks to wind your little one down for bed and make the most of your evenings. It doesn't feel as depressing when you finish work because it's still daylight!

Atmosphere:

Summer is the season of festivals, events and BBQs. There are lots of things you can do with your baby and lots of activities for them to try.

Tips for Summer Travel:

Stay Hydrated:

Keep your baby hydrated. Make sure you are both drinking plenty of water, especially if you're spending time outside in the sun.

Sun Protection:

As we know, babies have very sensitive skin and they need sun cream, sun hats and light airy clothes. Keep as much of their skin out of the sun as you can.

Seek Shade Often:

Stay out of the sun during the hottest part of the day and make sure that you regularly take your baby indoors for breaks from the sun.

Autumn:

My new favourite season since having Evelyn. The weather is milder, the colours are great, everywhere is getting cosy and red wine is socially acceptable once again.

What to Expect:

Changing Leaves:

Babies will be fascinated by the change of the leaves and the trees during the autumn season. Evelyn collects leaves and puts them in my pockets. She also has a fascination with pinecones and stones, so autumn is a great season for her.

Cooler Temperatures:

The weather is cooler but usually still sunny enough for babies to be outside and go on autumnal walks in the park. You can even take them pumpkin picking to a local farm. They won't have a clue what's going on, but you'll enjoy it even if they don't.

Tips for Autumn Travel:

Dress for the Weather:

Depending on where you go it could be quite cold or still very warm, so prepare for all eventualities and layer your baby up. Suncream may still be necessary!

Bring a Blanket for your Pram:

You may not need the full footmuff for your pram in the autumn, but you may need a soft, warm blanket to keep your baby warm during any outdoor activities.

Winter:

The most magical time of the year and the one where you must bundle your baby up in many layers.

What to Expect:

Snow:

Travelling in winter is the perfect opportunity to visit somewhere that is snowy and festive. A personal favourite of mine is Bruges. It is such a festive place and if you're there when it's snowing, it's quite something. Your baby will be mesmerised by snow and the twinkling lights.

Festive Atmosphere:

You have an opportunity to show your baby the spirit of the festive season with markets, opportunities to see real reindeer at farms as well as the magic of the lights and decorations all around you that will make your trip unforgettable. Seeing the fireworks on New Year's Eve will be fascinating for your little one, if you dare to keep them up that late!

Indoor Activities:

Winter is the ideal time to pursue indoor activities like Christmas baking or cosying up with a hot chocolate by the fire with your baby.

Tips for Winter Travel:

Layers:

Keep your baby warm and cosy and dress them in layers that trap heat but make sure the clothing still allows for easy movement and you can easily change a nappy. I went through a stage of putting Evelyn in tights and complicated jumpsuits and it was a nightmare when I needed to change her.

Flexibility:

Changes in weather mean changes in plans. Flights and activities can be delayed or cancelled. Have alternative activities in mind and consider alternative routes to airports in bad weather in case trains and buses are also delayed.

Chapter 20

Long Term Travel & Working Remotely

If you're looking for long-term travel with a baby, that's amazing. It will offer countless opportunities for exploration, growth, and unforgettable experiences.

Whether you're planning to wander the world for a few months or set off on a year-long adventure, there's plenty to consider when travelling long-term with your baby.

Planning Your Long-Term Travels

Before you jet off into the sunset, ensure that you do some careful planning to ensure a smooth and enjoyable journey for you and your baby.

Destinations:
Research potential destinations to find places that are baby-friendly, safe, and offer the experiences you're looking for.

Accommodation:

Opt for accommodation that offer separate living and sleeping areas. This allows you to work in one room while your baby naps in another.

Look for family-friendly accommodation options like serviced apartments, long term rentals, or hotels with baby amenities. If you book month long stays or more on places like Airbnb, a lot of places tend to offer discounts. When we stayed in France for the month, we got 30% off the cost for booking it for a longer period of time. Even if you're not doing exactly a month or two, it can be worth extending the dates of the stay to unlock these discounts even if you're checking out a few days or a week earlier.

Healthcare Considerations:

Familiarise yourself with healthcare options and vaccination requirements for each destination, and ensure your baby is up to date on vaccinations before you go. Consider whether your stay is going to follow over the dates when the next vaccinations are due.

If your baby requires any specific medication, make sure that you will have enough for the period you are away and discuss this with your GP as necessary.

Packing Essentials:

Pack light because you'll have access to amenities like washing machines but don't forget the essentials like baby gear and any specific items your baby needs.

Working Remotely on the Road

Working remotely while travelling allows you to sustain your adventures while maintaining your career or income stream. Here's how to make it work for you and your baby:

Create a Routine:

Wherever possible, try to establish a routine that balances work commitments with baby care, ensuring you have dedicated time for both.

Flexible Work Arrangements:

It may help to negotiate flexible work arrangements with your employer or consider freelance work that allows you to set your own hours. Make the most of annual leave so that you have an opportunity to work and explore, this allows you to extend your trips and that is how I tend to organise my trips to get maximum time away.

Remote Work Essentials:

First things first, you need to set up a mobile office that's adaptable on the move.

Invest in reliable technology and equipment like a lightweight laptop and good quality, durable case. Don't forget essentials like chargers (as well as a spare if you have room). Consider adapters used in your location and a portable mouse if necessary.

Noise-cancelling headphones are also a worthwhile investment for joining meetings and calls on the go in locations that may be a bit louder than usual.

You will, of course, need a smartphone (ideally one with a data plan that you can hotspot from in-case of a drop in Wi-Fi). You may prefer to use a portable Wi-Fi hotspot to stay connected and productive on the go.

Make sure your accommodation has a solid Wi-Fi connection to avoid any last-minute stress when working and unable to join meetings.

Protect your data with a VPN. It's crucial for secure connections, especially when using public Wi-Fi and

Consider whether your organisation has any barriers to remote working. For example, many financial institutions can have limitations on where you can access their networks remotely. Always have backups—cloud storage is your friend.

Navigating Day-to-Day Life on the Road

Living a digital nomad lifestyle with your baby comes with its own set of challenges (and rewards). Here are some tips for navigating day-to-day life on the road:

Office:

One of the many perks of working remotely is that your office" can be just about anywhere.

Cafés and Restaurants:

Many places are incredibly welcoming to families. Look for cafés with play areas or outdoor seating where your baby can safely toddle around while you work and can keep an eye on them.

Parks and Gardens:

Similarly, weather permitting, parks can be a great place to set up your office for the day. You can spread out a blanket, let your baby explore, and get some work done in the fresh air.

Co-Working Spaces:

In the new era of remote working, a growing number of cities offer co-working spaces, some of which offer child-friendly facilities, child-minding services or partnerships with local childcare providers. The Additional Resources chapter in this book gives more information about these spaces.

Juggling Work Hours and Quality Time

This is a tough one. If your job allows, embrace flexibility. Work during your baby's nap times, early mornings, or evenings. Split your workday into chunks and be prepared to adapt on the go.

Keep a stash of toys, books, and apps to keep your little one entertained. Don't underestimate the power of a good walk. Get your steps in and put your baby in the pram. You can catch up on calls while they sleep. This is something that always works for me if Evelyn won't go down for a nap and I have important calls to join.

Community Engagement:

Use social media and other platforms to connect with other travelling families or local parent groups to share tips, advice, and support.

Staying Productive on the Road

Maintaining productivity on the move is a challenge, one I'm still trying to master, but it is possible with a bit of strategy:

Prioritise Tasks:

Use tools like Trello, Asana or, (my favourite) an old-fashioned to-do list, to prioritise your tasks. Focus on what absolutely needs to be done and tackle those first.

Set Boundaries:

It's easy to blur the lines between work and leisure when you're abroad, especially when you're working from home and can lose track of time.

Set clear boundaries for your work hours and stick to them as much as possible. When you're off the clock, be present with your baby and try not to do any additional work!

Communicate:

Keep open lines of communication with your colleagues and clients. Let them know your availability and any potential time zone differences.

Managing Logistics and Practicalities

Travelling long-term with a baby requires careful planning and organisation to manage logistics and practicalities effectively. Here are some ideas on how to stay on top of things:

Budgeting:

Create a budget that accounts for travel expenses, accommodation, food, healthcare, equipment and any additional costs associated with travelling with a baby.

Transport:

Research transportation options and plan your routes carefully to ensure smooth and safe travel with your baby. Ensure you will be able to access Wi-Fi as needed around your work schedule.

Working remotely is such a good opportunity to travel and see more of the world, if you have the option, do it whilst your baby is young.

Chapter 21

What Next?

As we look to the future, Evelyn and I have set our sights on an ambitious goal: to visit 24 countries by the time she's 2 years old. It's born from a desire to instil in her a love for adventure, a curiosity for different cultures, and a spirit of exploration as well as my love for a challenge.

Discovering Myself as a Passport Parent

I've learnt that I am more Passport Parent then Helicopter Parent and on our travels over this past year, I've discovered strengths I never knew I had and faced challenges I never imagined. Being a parent has pushed me out of my comfort zone, tested my patience, taught me resilience and made me the happiest I have ever been.

I've learned to adapt to new environments, embrace uncertainty, and find joy in the simplest of moments – whether it's watching Evelyn splash in the ocean for the first time or watching her excitement on her first camel ride.

As I reflect on the journey we've been on, I'm filled with gratitude for the experiences we've shared, even if Evelyn may not remember them.

To all the parents out there considering adventures with their little ones: go for it. You will not regret it.

As you've seen throughout this journey, the difficulty has increased the older that Evelyn has gotten. Each time we think we've cracked it; a new level of difficulty is unlocked. We are constantly challenged. This, I guess, is parenthood. A constant evolution.

Evelyn has been to 18 countries in her first 18 months, and we'd like to take her on a longer haul flight before she is two (and it gets a lot more expensive!). We are looking at Thailand, having had several friends and family visit there in recent months who have recommended it to us. Thailand was a destination I did consider when I was pregnant, before we settled on Canada and the USA. Now that Evelyn is older, I think she would really enjoy and get more out of a longer trip to somewhere that is unlike anywhere she's visited so far.

Aside from our plans for a more exotic trip further afield, Evelyn and I are going on an extended trip around Europe in the coming months and we will be visiting the Czech Republic, Denmark, Sweden, Switzerland and Germany to name a few.

The adventure continues.

Conclusion

So, here we are at the end of the first leg of this journey. You've seen the highs and lows of globe-trotting with a one-year-old. If you've stuck with me this far, well done. You're either a glutton for punishment or you're seriously contemplating taking your baby on adventure. Either way, I appreciate you enormously.

Let's not mince words: travelling with a tiny human is not all sunsets and selfies. There were moments when I seriously questioned my sanity. Sleepless nights in unfamiliar places and tantrums in the middle of airport floors. It's a lot but it's worth it.

For every meltdown we endured, there was a moment of pure magic: seeing my daughter's face light up at her first sight of the ocean, hearing her say 'WOW!' to every gondola we passed in Venice, and watching her curiosity grow with every new experience. These highs have a way of making you forget the lows, or at least making them into a funny anecdote to share.

Now, let's get real. Waiting for the perfect time to travel with your little one? Surprise: It doesn't exist. There will always be reasons to postpone—work commitments, financial constraints, fear of the unknown, waiting until they're older and more 'manageable'.

But if I've learnt anything over the past few years: life really doesn't wait, and babies grow so quickly. Life is far too short for you to stay at home: get out there and explore the world.

Recommendations

Throughout this book I have spoken about booking transport, accommodation, ordering food to our apartments, booking excursions and generally getting around these places that we've been to.

Below you will find a non-exhaustive list of websites, companies and Apps that I use time and time again that I think could be beneficial to you when doing your travel research before you go and for when you reach your destination.

Now, a lot of these I am sure you are already familiar with and there will be some that may be new to you. There will also be countless others that I haven't come across yet and ones that you may prefer to the ones below. This is intended to be a guide not a bible.

Accommodation:

Airbnb

This is my go-to. It is great for travelling with little ones where you need space for cots and all the things that come with them. It is invaluable having a kitchen for sterilising, making bottles and making baby friendly food. Lots of Airbnbs we book ask me if I needed a changing table, highchair or cot for our stay which really helps us travel light. It is also really good where you don't want to go to bed at the same time as your baby, you aren't limited in the same way that you can be in a hotel where you're sleeping in the same room as your baby with nowhere else to go!

Transport:

Omio

This App is fantastic for booking train travel all over the world. It allows you to book trains in advance or very last minute and they're available instantly on your phone for scanning. You can filter by fastest or most direct route, price and timings. This App has been a life saver for me in so many places.

Uber

Obviously not every country or city will have Uber but a lot of them do and we use Uber a lot where we need to get from A to B with Evelyn and all our things. Particularly if we have just arrived in a new place and it's late, we are tired and we just want to get to our accommodation. Some places have their own local taxis linked to the Uber app and they can often work out cheaper than an Uber car itself. With Uber and apps similar, the benefit is knowing it's a licensed driver and that the fee and route are agreed in advance. Uber fares can be higher in some countries where it isn't as popular and in those countries you might have a bit of a wait on your hands. Electric scooters and bikes are also available on Uber in some locations. Uber Pool is available in certain locations if you're happy to share your cab with a stranger. Personally, I am always partial to an Uber Pool in London because, depending on the time of night, you can sometimes find yourself in a carpool karaoke situation with the driver and the other passengers belting I'm a Survivor by Destiny's Child out of your window as you zoom past the Thames.

Bolt

If I get somewhere and discover that they don't have Uber, I check Bolt. If you haven't used Bolt before, it is very similar to Uber and it is used in some countries and cities where Uber is not available (and also in addition to Uber in many places). I used Bolt in Slovakia, Malta, Portugal, Denmark, Croatia and Austria as I struggled to get Uber in these locations at the time. It can be hit and miss with the wait times. They also have options to use the electric scooters via the App if you're so inclined.

CityMapper

This App is brilliant and is in the majority of major cities. You can easily get from A to B using various modes of transport with this App. It gives you several options for travel (bus, metro, train etc.) and it even tells you which carriage to get on for an easier transition out of the stations. Most of the major cities are on there and they are regularly updating it with new ones and do polls quite often to see where people want them to cover next.

Rome2Rio

I use Rome2Rio's site to plan my route when I am looking at going from country to country. When I went from Austria to Slovakia I used this to work out the easiest and best way to do the trip. It gives you the option for inputting multiple destinations and is a very useful tool. It tells you the cost and duration of the journey depending whether you do taxi, train, car etc. and can be very helpful for working out timings and costs ahead of a trip.

SkyScanner

Now I am sure you are all familiar with SkyScanner but it gets an honourable mention for being the only tool I use to book flights. It gives you so many options for times, prices, airlines and direct or indirect flights. Again, it has a multiple destination option to help you work out the quickest and or cheapest way to get several flights.

My favourite thing to do with SkyScanner is to pick a month I want to go away and use the destination: everywhere tool. It then shows me the cheapest options for that month which can get you a really good deal for flights if you are flexible. You can also put specific dates in if you want to and it'll show you the cheapest destinations available for those dates.

The only thing to be wary of is booking through third party companies like Trip.com and others as some of the airlines will charge you a small fee when you come to check in and you'll have to do identity checks before the airline lets you validate your booking and check in.

Experiences

Viator

I have used Viator on multiple occasions and have never had a bad excursion with them. It's under the TripAdvisor umbrella so I always like to use this for the added protection that they offer as a consumer. They offer thousands of experiences, day trips, private airport transfers and the like in countries all over the world. You can search by destination and filter by type of experience and number of people and your travel dates.

Trips I have booked through there include a camel ride and entry into the pyramids in Cairo, kayaking in Portofino, whale watching in California, sunset boat trips in Amalfi, wine and food tours in Paris and many more. You can do helicopter rides, private tours and even full day and night trips from one city or country to another.

They give you a detailed itinerary, what to bring, what's included and what isn't along with pick-up and drop-off information. It's very flexible and allows you to book now, pay later which is perfect if you haven't quite ironed out all of your trip details yet but don't want to miss out. It's also easy to amend the date of your excursions right up until 24 hours before usually. All of the trips I have been on through Viator have been fantastic and I definitely recommend this one to any of you.

Get Your Guide

This is another App I use that is very similar to Viator above but offers some different trips and locations. Sometimes one of the Apps will have availability on your dates and one won't so it's useful to have a couple of options in case your trip is sold out one of them for the dates you need. The App is really easy to use, it gives a lot of detailed information on the trip, and I would recommend that you download it.

Deliveries

Whilst we all have the best intentions to go out and sample local cuisines each night, my travel experiences have showed me that sometimes you need to cut your losses. Some evenings you have no choice but to put an overtired baby to bed early and order in before putting your overtired self to bed too. Most of these Apps you'll have heard of before but some you might not have. There are so many available for all different countries so these are just a few that I have used:

UberEats

A lot of major cities have UberEats and it's great for a range of different cuisines and even getting groceries delivered if you can't get to the local supermarket.

Glovo

This App is popular in Spain, Mallorca, Italy and Portugal as well as many other countries. It works the same as Deliveroo or UberEats but you can also order things from shops such as clothing stores, pharmacies, cosmetics stores, toy shops and homeware stores. It was revolutionary to me when I first discovered it. Great service and you can track your rider but sometimes there are quite high delivery fees and minimum order spends depending on your country.

Wolt

This is mostly a food delivery service like UberEats but is used in Malta, Hungary and Slovakia and many more.

JustEat

There are lots of different versions of JustEat that vary country to country and it can be a great way of sourcing local restaurants if you're unable to get there in person.

Final Word

I hope that you have found this book useful and that it has given you an idea of how travelling might look for you and your family.

Whilst I have made some recommendations in the preceding chapter for the various places that we have travelled to, I have also created a series of helpful e-guides for several of these countries and others that we have travelled to since this book was written. These guides will give you more detailed information about where to stay, how to get around, places of interest as well as good bars and restaurants and the best time of year to travel depending on what you're looking for.

It can be difficult to know where to start when planning a trip with your little one, particularly if you're thinking about the logistics of doing day trips to other places. My e-guides will give you some great ideas and some useful information for all of your travelling questions to allow you to go on many unforgettable trips for both you and your little one.

Appendix 1: Travel Checklist

Embarking on a journey with your baby requires careful planning and organisation. Use this handy travel checklist to help you stay organised:

Before You Go:

☐ Check passports and visas (if travelling internationally).

☐ Pack travel documents (tickets, itinerary, accommodation reservations, hire car documents etc.).

☐ Ensure you have travel insurance that covers your baby.

☐ Confirm healthcare arrangements and vaccination requirements for your destination.

Packing Essentials:

☐ Clothing: Onesies/bodysuits, sleepwear, tops, bottoms, socks, hats, sweaters/jumpers, jackets/coats, etc.

☐ Nappy-changing Essentials: Nappies, baby wipes, nappy rash cream, changing pad/mat, nappy disposal bags, etc.

☐ Feeding Supplies: Bottles/nursing supplies, formula/breast milk, baby food/snacks, muslins, bibs, etc.

☐ Sleeping Gear: Travel cot/portable crib, baby blankets/sleeping bags, baby monitor, white noise machine, etc.

☐ Baby Gear: Lightweight pram, baby carrier/sling, car seat (if applicable), travel highchair, etc.

☐ Health and Safety: Baby first-aid kit, baby suncream, baby insect repellent, hand sanitiser, etc.

☐ Entertainment and Comfort: Baby toys, board books, baby blanket, portable baby play mat, etc.

☐ Miscellaneous: Baby's passport/ID (if travelling internationally),

On the Go:

☐ Pack snacks and drinks for your baby.

☐ Carry a change of clothes for your baby in case of spillages or accidents.

☐ Bring baby's favourite comfort items (dummy, teddy etc.)

☐ Keep baby essentials easily accessible during travel (nappies, wipes, feeding supplies, etc.).

During Your Trip:

☐ Stick to your baby's routine as much as possible (feeding, napping, bedtime, etc.).

☐ Allow for plenty of rest and downtime for you and your baby.

☐ Take breaks during travel for feeding, changing, napping and coffee.

☐ Be flexible and patient – travel with a baby may not always go according to plan, but that's all part of the adventure!

After Your Trip:

☐ Check your belongings and make sure you haven't left anything behind.

☐ Reflect on your travel experience and make sure to have some photos from your trip printed for your baby's memory book or for photobooks in your home.

☐ Start planning your next baby adventure – the world is waiting!

Appendix 2: Sample Packing List

Here's a sample packing list to help you ensure you have everything you need for a smooth and enjoyable journey with your little one:

Clothing:

- Onesies/bodysuits (7-10)

- Sleepsuits/pyjamas (7-10)

- T-shirts/tops (5-7)

- Bottoms (5-7)

- Jumpers/cardigans (2-3)

- Socks (7-10 pairs)

- Hats (sun hat, warm hat)

- Bibs (5-7)

- Swimsuit (if applicable)

- Jacket/coat (weather-dependent)

Nappy-changing Essentials:

- Nappies (either enough to get you to your destination and the first day until you buy some more or enough for the duration of your trip, plus extras)

- Baby wipes

- Nappy rash cream

- Changing pad/mat

- Nappy disposal bags

Feeding Supplies:

- Bottles/nursing supplies

- Formula (if applicable)

- Baby food/snacks (if applicable)

- Muslins

- Bibs

Sleeping Gear:

- Travel cot/portable crib

- Baby blankets/sleeping bags

- Baby monitor (if applicable)

- White noise machine (if needed)

Baby Gear:

- Lightweight stroller/pushchair

- Baby carrier/sling
- Car seat (if applicable)
- Travel highchair (if needed)
- Portable baby bathtub (if needed)

Health and Safety:

- Baby first-aid kit (including thermometer, Calpol, teething gel, etc.)
- Baby suncream
- Baby insect repellent
- Hand sanitiser
- Baby's toiletries

Entertainment and Comfort:

- Baby toys
- Board books
- Baby blanket
- Portable baby play mat

Miscellaneous:

- Baby's passport/ID (if travelling internationally)

- Travel documents (tickets, itinerary, accommodation reservations, etc.)

- Baby's favourite comfort items (dummy, teddy etc.)

- Portable highchair/booster seat (if needed)

- Packing cubes

- Small backpack for the day to keep essential baby items in

Notes:

- Remember to pack according to the climate and weather conditions of your destination.

- Consider the duration of your trip and pack enough supplies to last the entire journey.

- Check airline regulations and restrictions regarding baby gear and luggage allowances.

- Don't forget to leave room in your luggage for souvenirs and wine collected along the way! I collect baubles from everywhere we go and it's so nice putting them on the tree each Christmas and remembering our trips.

Acknowledgments

A lot has gone into this book, it has been a labour of love over the past year and I couldn't have done it without the help and input of several wonderful people.

Evelyn, for turning my world upside down in the very best way and teaching me that there is magic in the chaos. I love you.

Mike, for coming on every trip and going along with all my wild ideas for the next one. For successfully navigating us from A to B and for getting that van around Portugal and for being an amazing Dad to Evelyn.

Mumsy, for encouraging me to explore the world even though some of my adventures with Evelyn terrify you. You are my biggest supporter and I love you millions.

Grandma, for passing your adventurous streak to me and for always being supportive of our travels. Thank you for never getting bored of the photos we bombard you with and for inspiring us to keep travelling when we see your adventures! We love you.

Becki, for being my partner in crime and my better half. For always being game for a trip and a spritz, for encouraging me to write this book and being the best Auntie to Evelyn.

Printed in Great Britain
by Amazon